FROM IRON FIST TO INVISIBLE HAND

FROM IRON FIST

TO INVISIBLE HAND

The Uneven Path of

Telecommunications

Reform in China

Irene S. Wu

STANFORD UNIVERSITY PRESS
Stanford, California

Stanford University Press
Stanford, California
© 2009 by the Board of Trustees of the Leland Stanford Junior University.
All rights reserved.

Printed in the United States of America on acid-free, archival-quality paper

Library of Congress Cataloging-in-Publication Data

Wu, Irene S.
    From iron fist to invisible hand : the uneven path of telecommunications reform in China / Irene S. Wu.
        p. cm.
    Includes bibliographical references and index.
    ISBN 978-0-8047-5962-5 (cloth : alk. paper)
    1. Telecommunication policy—China.   2. Telecommunication—China—History.   3. Freedom of information—China.   4. Trade regulation—China.
I. Title.
    HE8425.W8 2009
    384.0951—dc22   2008014764

Typeset by Westchester Book Group in 10/13.5 Sabon

For my parents, Chuen-Shiong and Lily Wu, and my sister, Tina

Contents

Illustrations

Tables

Figures

Preface

The underlying assumption of this book is that the objective of government policy, ultimately, is to improve the quality of life of its citizens. While writing it, I was an official in the U.S. government at the Federal Communications Commission, the regulatory agency for telephones and television. Therefore, I am intimately familiar with the pressures and compromises necessary in policy work. Consequently, I have both sympathy and empathy for my colleagues in China as they alternately succeed and fail with their policies. I continue to have a high regard for them and their work.

Also, I wish to thank the dozens of experts in China who shared with me their insights at length. They cannot be named now, but I look forward to a time when no one would worry if they were.

While working on this research, I had many advisors. Especially, I thank my advisor David Lampton, as well as Anne Thurston, Scott Barrett, Robert Pepper, and Karl Jackson for their suggestions. Ernest Wilson and Peter Cowhey provided cogent comments that clarified and shaped the ideas in this book. Dan Wright read through the entire manuscript at a critical moment. As I mentioned earlier, I worked at the FCC while writing on weekends and on leave. I thank my many friends there who either by doing more or asking less, enabled me to get on with this research. In the end, however, this book reflects a personal, not an official view, and I am fully responsible for its remaining flaws.

Funding for the field work came from Johns Hopkins University's School of Advanced International Studies and from the National Security Education Program, now known as the Boren Fellowship. From Georgetown University, I received a research fellowship from the Yahoo! International Values, Communications, Technology, and Global Internet Fund, which enabled me to revise and finish the manuscript. My thanks to all these organizations for their support. Also, I thank Muriel Bell, Stacy Wagner, Kirstin Olson, Carolyn Brown, Jessica Walsh, and Joa Suarez at Stanford University Press; Debbie Masi at Westchester Book Group; and all the others who kindly guided me and pushed this book to completion.

Finally, for their love, I thank my parents, Chuen-Shiong and Lily Wu, and my sister, Tina, and to them this book is dedicated.

Irene S. Wu
Washington, D.C.
April 2008

Abbreviations

3G	third generation wireless telecommunications
AFP	Agence France-Presse
APEC	Asia Pacific Economic Cooperation
AT&T	American Telephone and Telegraph
BT	British Telecom
CCF	Chinese-Chinese-Foreign investment arrangement
CCTV	China Central Television
CDMA	code division multiplex access
CITEL	Comisión Interamericana de Telecomunicaciones (Organization of American States)
DGT	Directorate General of Telecommunications (same title in China and Taiwan)
DSL	digital subscriber line
FCC	Federal Communications Commission (United States)
GSM	global system mobile
IDD	international direct dial
IP	Internet protocol
IPO	initial public offering
ITU	International Telecommunications Union
MCI	Microwave Communications Incorporated

MEI	Ministry of Electronics Industry (China)
MII	Ministry of Information Industry (China)
MOFTEC	Ministry of Foreign Trade and Economic Cooperation
MPHPT	Ministry of Home Affairs, Posts, and Telecom munications (Japan)
MPT	Ministry of Posts and Telecommunications (same title used in China and Japan)
MRFT	Ministry of Radio, Film, and Television (China)
NTT	Nippon Telephone and Telegraph
OECD	Organisation of Economic Co-operation and Development
Ofcom	Office of Communications (United Kingdom)
Oftel	Office of Telecommunications (United Kingdom)
PHS	personal handyphone service
PLA	Peoples' Liberation Army (China)
PRC	Peoples' Republic of China
SARFT	State Administration for Radio, Film, and Television (China)
SPDC	State Planning and Development Commission (China)
WTO	World Trade Organization

FROM IRON FIST TO INVISIBLE HAND

1   From Iron Fist to Somewhat Invisible Hand

In 1980 there were 2 million telephones in China, by 2000 there were 230 million, and by 2005 there were 744 million. How did this happen? The simple story is that the government abandoned the command economy and embraced a socialist brand of market economy, and telephones boomed in China like they did in most countries around the world. The back story, however, is more complex. As a capital-intensive network industry where just getting competing operators to agree to complete each other's calls often requires government guidelines, telecommunications service markets are characterized by extensive regulation, even in the most liberal of economies. For a socialist market in transition, the shift from iron fist to invisible hand is challenging. In China, the liberalization of the telecommunications market is a prime example of the planned economy discarded and the piecemeal construction of an uneasy foundation for a rules-based market economy. To add a further twist to this change, the telecommunications network in modern society is the common carrier of ideas and information. Because ideas and information are not ideologically neutral, alongside China's liberalization efforts for the network are companion efforts to control the content of communications across the network. Although many of the challenges China faces in liberalizing its telecom market mirror those of other countries, China's tactics for regulating the content of communications services are unique.

As Barry Naughton and Dali Yang document in their recent book, *Holding China Together: Diversity and National Integration in the Post-Deng Era*, there are two main strands in the current research on the Chinese economy. One strand documents the deconstruction of centralized national power and the disintegration of the economic and social governance, focusing on the rise of provincial and local authorities, rampant problems of corruption, the emergence of informal or illegal markets, and other developments that suggest that the fabric holding together the nation is torn. The second strand documents the rise of China as a great power, highlighting its rapid economic growth and its share of the global market, whether in exports or imports, in either goods or services.[1] As Naughton and Yang argue in *Holding China Together* and Yang argues again in a separate book, *Remaking the Chinese Leviathan: Market Transformation and the Politics of Governance in China*, neither is the national state disappearing in China, nor is it yet a great power, but rather it is still in the midst of transformation. In some respects, the central state's goal is to limit the role of government; in other respects, the central state's goal is to extend its power—for example, in building regulatory frameworks to oversee industries that were previously run as part of the government.[2] The telecommunications sector is one of these industries in which the role of the state is in metamorphosis.

Currently, there are two major explanations for what drives economic reform. As put forward in 1988 and 1992 by Lieberthal, Oksenberg, and Lampton, one is that government bureaucracies vie for resources, prestige, and authority, and the final policy decisions that emanate from the government are essentially the negotiated compromises among these parties.[3] Although this explanation for Chinese government policy has fallen out of favor recently as more of the economy escapes central planning, in the relatively highly regulated sector of telecommunications, it is actually still quite relevant. A second explanation put forward by Barry Naughton is that once unleashed, the economic reform process in China is fundamentally self-reinforcing. A state-owned monopoly is broken, new actors enter the market, prices begin to reflect market supply and demand, state-owned enterprises must adjust to compete, and the cycle begins once again.[4]

These two explanations actually nest one in the other, as Xu Yi-chong argues in a study of China's electricity reform.[5] Telecom reform also bears out this argument, as does an examination of other network sectors in China, such as banking and airlines. At the heart of each of these sectors is a former monopoly that is divided into smaller enterprises. However, these smaller enterprises remain giants in the sector compared with private companies that may have entered. The giants often represent the commercial interests of various government ministries, all of which must arrive at some consensus for any major policy reform to go forward. These bureaucracies compete to achieve policies that are most advantageous for themselves and the industries they represent. However, nonstate forces are continually changing the context in which these bureaucratic negotiations take place; they are the forces that push forward the reform cycle. Markets expand, innovative services arise, and consumers become more demanding. Policy reform, often in the case of network industries appearing in the form of increased government regulation, is required to meet the demands of the new context. If this does not happen, failures follow: power shortages occur, phone calls fail to connect, bank lending dries up, and planes fall out of the sky. Those familiar with life in China in the last twenty-five years will recognize all these travails. These highly regulated industries differ from others, such as manufacturing, where in a liberalized market the hand of government is nearly invisible.

Up until 1994, there was a monopoly in telecommunications services; competition since then has brought more services and cheaper prices.[6] The government has allowed new firms to enter the market by two means: on rare occasions, by issuing a license to a new firm, and, more frequently, by slicing up an existing operator into several bits. Only a few countries in the world, such as the United States and Brazil, have been as vigorous as China in divesting incumbent telecom operators. The Chinese government split China Telecom once in 1999 into four companies, and again in 2002 into two companies. In 2007, rumors swirled again about the possibility that China Unicom might be split. Past reorganizations of companies by the government have created expectations of future ones.[7]

In this regard, telecommunications policy reform has mirrored reform in several other sectors of the Chinese economy. In the 1980s, the airline monopoly was devolved into regional operating bureaus, and new companies were permitted to enter.[8] Also in the 1980s, the People's

Bank of China was designated as the central bank, and four other banks were separated from it.[9] In the electricity sector, change occurred more recently. After a period of consolidation, the main State Power Corporation was split into several regional units in 2002.[10] Although this divestiture of national monopolies is unusual compared with other countries, within China it is a regular phenomenon. This is shown in detail in Chapter 4, which explores the entry of new firms into the market and discusses the contending forces and dramatic ministerial struggles that led the government to break up China Telecom twice.

Paralleling the dismantling of monopolies is the reform of regulatory structures. Between 1990 and 2000, the government offices with responsibility for communications services went from three ministries to one ministry, plus one administration with reduced status; the ministry that won the battle was separated from the telecom operator, reducing its staff of hundreds of thousands to a couple of hundred. These transformations of the regulatory structure represented victory for the telecommunications ministry over the electronics manufacturing ministry and, to a certain extent, over the television and radio ministry. In the meantime, technically above the fray but still deeply involved in it, were various transformations of offices within the State Council, a higher government body than the ministries with oversight in this policy area. Competition among government ministries to launch their own operators into the telecom market was fierce because the market was so lucrative. In other sectors of the economy, similar regulatory transformations have occurred. In the airline sector, the Civil Aviation Administration of China (CAAC) was separated from airline carriers in 1985.[11] In 1995, a new banking law separated commercial banking from the central bank, the People's Bank of China, and established the China Banking Regulatory Commission.[12] In electricity, the State Economic and Trade Commission was established as a comprehensive regulatory body for the sector in 1997.[13]

Furthermore, recent regulatory reform of network industries is not unique to China. Worldwide, there has been a rise in regulatory agencies, reflecting a fundamental reassessment of the usefulness of regulatory oversight for some aspects of economic development. In 1990, there were only thirteen telecom regulatory agencies in the world;[14] by 2005, there were over 130 such authorities.[15] This is part of a broader global trend: the rise of regulatory agencies in a range of countries across a range of sectors, such as banking, water, and power.[16] Chapter 3, on the evolution of the policymaker, places the rise of the Ministry of Information Industry in the context of broad administrative reform in China and evolving international consensus on good regulatory practice.

For a telecommunications regulator, once a monopoly is broken, one of its first tasks is to deal with prices. At the wholesale level, this is known as interconnection. Interconnection policy governs the settlement of traffic and money between operators. When a subscriber of Operator A wants to telephone a subscriber of Operator B, this is possible only because the interconnection regime in the market governs how and at what price that telephone call will be handed off from one operator to the next. Monopoly markets have no need for an interconnection regime. Therefore, the government's decision to move from a single to multiple operator environment means a new interconnection regime has to be constructed. In recent years, the interconnection regime in China has been evolving with difficulties. China Telecom, as many incumbent telecommunications operators do, resisted interconnection with competitors in order to protect its profits. The two state-led breakups of China Telecom rose in part out of the company's unwillingness to comply with the interconnection regime. The success of the interconnection regime thus depends on the ability and will of the regulator to intervene and reflects the government's commitment to a competitive telecommunications market.

Although when compared with other countries China's interconnection regime is still rudimentary and has considerable room to evolve, it is quite advanced when compared with policy developments in other sectors of the economy. As of 2005, interconnection between regional power grids had not been resolved. The implication is that because use of natural resources cannot be optimized over large areas and because major generation sources are separated from major usage areas, more investment in power generation is required if grids remain separate rather than interconnected.[17] Although interconnection in telecommunications appears more advanced than in China's other network sectors, as will be shown in Chapter 6, one of the issues at the heart of competition policy is the ministry's struggle to enforce its regulations on operators more accustomed to blunt instruments of government power than to following administrative rules.

Although in many respects the telecom sector is similar to other network sectors in China, it differs in that its service is often not ideologically neutral. Electricity in and of itself is not rightist or leftist. Money transferred from one bank to another is not ideologically fraught, although the lending of it might be. In telecommunications, the service being transmitted is information. An essential aspect of political power is controlling the ideological debate, which depends significantly on the communications of those who govern to those who are governed. Although such sectors as electricity, the airlines, and banking are all politically sensitive industries, telecommunications is especially so, and the limits on nonstate and foreign actors in the market have been more strict in the telecom sector than in others. Compared with other countries, China has been especially keen to involve its propaganda apparatus in the development of the communications network, an approach with long-term political implications. In other sectors, such as electricity, the airlines, and banking, there seem to be no parallels.

For example, new technology has enabled both cable television and telecommunications networks to offer quite similar services. Both can provide telephone and Internet service; in many countries, television service is available over telecom networks. In China, the convergence of cable television and telecommunications networks touches on questions of programming and content, which are the province of the State Administration for Radio, Film, and Television (SARFT) and the Chinese Communist Party's Propaganda Department, responsible for ideological discipline nationwide. Whether telecommunications interests will let the SARFT companies enter the telecommunications service market without concessions similar to those allowing telecommunications companies into broadcasting remains unclear. This tension curtails China's telecommunications industry from straightforwardly taking advantage of the latest technology developments. Chapter 3 examines the nexus between China's communications market and the government's ideological framework.

Reflecting its interest in controlling the content of communications, the state retains management of the telecommunications networks. Although the government has allowed some competition, only state-controlled operators are permitted to compete. Furthermore, China's approach toward foreigners interested in the communications services is to attract maximum capital while minimizing managerial influence. Prior to joining the World Trade Organization (WTO), the Chinese government permitted certain limited foreign investment in telecommunication services in 1994 in China Unicom. However, the government forced out these investors beginning in 1997. Subsequently, China's commitments under the WTO agreement established a formal map of how limited foreign investment in telecommunications would be permitted over several years' time. Even the most open of China's commitments does not permit foreign control over network operations. Today, all foreign investment in China's major telecom operators has been portfolio investment through shares offered on foreign stock exchanges.

In contrast, in electricity, the airlines, and banking, entry requirements for private investors and for foreign investors in practice appear more relaxed. In the airline industry, foreign investors have been permitted to hold minority shares in carriers since 1994.[18] Purely privately owned carriers Okay, Spring, and United Eagle Airlines received licenses in 2004.[19] In the electricity sector, private and foreign investment has been permitted in principle since 1994; the first foreign investment occurred in 1996.[20] Although there are more restrictions on foreign investment in the electricity grid, foreign investment in electricity generation is encouraged. In banking, foreign investment is permitted in the four largest national banks. In 2005, large foreign banks and investment groups purchased significant, if minority, shares in both China Construction Bank and the Bank of China. Among smaller banks in China, joint ventures are common, and foreigners may have managerial influence, such as in the Shenzhen Development Bank, which has foreigners as both chairman and president.[21] In telecommunications, such extensive participation by foreign investors in management of carriers is not under consideration. Chapter 5 discusses in detail the deep ambivalence of the state in allowing outsiders to manage its communications networks.

The debates on China's regulatory reform, monopoly breakup, wholesale pricing, and foreign investment are all stories that largely focus on large bureaucracies negotiating with each other on the next policy step. However, it is also essential to examine how policy reforms have brought about changes in the larger context in which these negotiations were taking place, changes which themselves ultimately have a bearing on future reforms. In telecommunications, consistent with Naughton's theory, price reform is a key factor in propelling reforms in a self-reinforcing way. In addition, technological change has a similar effect, especially as a major factor in changing costs and, therefore, prices.

In principle, the government regulates the prices that consumers in China pay for voice telecommunications services. Usually, there is a single price or a single range of prices, which should apply nationwide for per minute local calls, domestic long distance calls, and international calls. Likewise, there are prescribed price ranges that consumers should be able to obtain for wireless service packages. General pricing rules are set in Beijing by the Ministry of Information Industry and are implemented at the provincial level by provincial communications administrations. To a significant degree, Beijing has been successful in moving away from a pricing regime that uses international and long distance calls to subsidize local calls, a major challenge not unique to China and an important step toward a competitive market. However, there is some evidence now that in some segments of the market, companies are offering service packages that more closely cater to the demands of consumers, rather than following the pricing rules set by the government. Although consumers may not be organized into a single lobbying group, by voting with their wallets they have an impact on policymaking.

A parallel example of the government's loss of control in another sector is the airline industry's price wars of the 1990s, once supply met demand for air travel. In 1998, for example, carriers began offering 40 percent discounts on domestic fares. The government's response was to ban discounts, increase ticket prices, and prohibit carriers from purchasing new aircraft for two years.[22] In electricity, user tariffs are set below cost, discouraging investment and contributing toward power shortages.[23] Tariffs in telecommunications in China were also once set below cost, but policy reforms in the 1990s enabled operators to recover investment costs, and network build-out expanded. The history of several network industries confirms Naughton and Yang's argument that once price reforms begin, they can become self-reinforcing. Chapter 7 is an overview of retail pricing of telecommunications services in China and provides insight into the future flexibility that will be required in regulation.

Technology is still changing quickly, and the regulator's ability to adapt to these changes affects the future development of the market. One such example is Internet Protocol (IP) telephony, which emerged in the late 1990s as a new technique for delivering voice signals over the telecommunications network. Only after losing a lawsuit and following considerable public discussion did the Ministry of Information Industry permit experimental launch of IP telephony service in China in 1999. When introduced, the service became cheap and popular very quickly and several companies competed to offer the service to the public. A second example is "Little Smart" wireless phones, an old but inexpensively deployed technology that was introduced to China in the late 1990s. This technology allowed an operator to provide consumers with a cheap wireless phone service built on the foundation of a wireline telecommunications network. The state's initial reaction was to ban the service, but in the face of its widespread popularity, the telecommunications ministry gradually ceased declaring it illegal.

In other sectors, popular resistance to regulatory constraints has also spawned informal markets. In electricity, when power is unreliable, companies invest in their own electricity generation.[24] In banking, when caps on interest rates force bank lending to dry up, non–bank lending by private parties to each other takes off.[25] When such unregulated parallel markets emerge prominently, the government must either adapt or look as if it has ceded authority in that economic sector. That risk is often an impetus for further reform. Chapter 8, on IP telephony and Little Smart service, takes a closer look at how technological change enables the growth of informal sectors that, in turn, force the liberalization of government policy.

Although a detailed comparative analysis across China's industry sectors is beyond the scope of this investigation, this study of the telecommunications market does contribute to an understanding of the nature of economic reform in these network industries, which are the lifeblood of modernizing economies. Through the next several chapters, a picture emerges of the policymaking scene in China, as encapsulated in Figure 1.1. The major actors are large bureaucratic organizations. In the

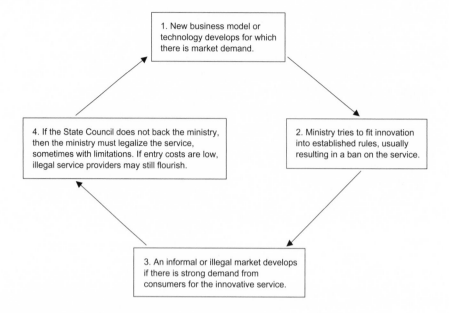

FIGURE 1.1 Government response to service innovation

communications area, these are still defined by specific industry interests. Other government organizations, such as the railway and the television bureaucracies, are backers of state-owned companies that compete with telecom ministry-backed operators. Each unit pursues its own interest, some economic and some ideological. The State Council is responsible for brokering compromises. However, outside this tight circle are forces that alter the relative strength and importance of the bureaucracies. Technical or business innovations that serve customers better can give some organizations a competitive advantage over others, altering the balance of power among actors negotiating for policy outcomes.

The data collected for these case studies are from individual interviews I conducted, from a variety of meetings and conferences, and from news media and academic publications in the United States and China, in both English and Chinese. Between 1996 and 2007, I worked in the International Bureau of Federal Communications Commission (FCC), the communications regulator for the United States, during which I led, organized, and participated in dozens of meetings with hundreds of Chinese officials and business people. All the views in this book, of course, are my own and do not reflect the views of the FCC. During three extended trips to China in 2002 and 2003, I conducted a series of interviews expressly for this book.

The last twenty-five years in China have been a period of enormous change in communications policy and regulation. These are the policies that govern the infrastructure on which ride cell phones, e-mail, and the whole range of Internet services. These services seem so new that it is possible to forget that they were preceded by a whole range of communications services—from message couriers to postal mail. Chapter 2 thus begins with a history of the telegraph in China, in which the concerns of today are certainly foreshadowed.

2 China's Telecommunications History

Seeking Control While Liberalizing to Modernize

Sometime after Hong Kong became a British colony following China's defeat in the Opium War of the 1840s, the British deployed submarine cables to link its empire by telegraph.[1] Messages from London to Hong Kong, which once took forty days, could be delivered within a few hours and sometimes within minutes.[2] China, which had lost not only Hong Kong but also several other port cities to foreign powers, greeted this technology with an uneven mix of interest and fear.[3] Chinese officials resisted all applications by foreigners to establish telegraph networks in China, although some officials saw this as a futile exercise. One prominent official, Li Hongzhang, well known for his support of modernization and innovation, in 1865 noted:

> The costs of telegraph lines are not great, and transmitting a message can be extremely fast. Foreigners have had their mind set on operating [telegraphs in China] for a long time. It is not clear whether, in the future, we can go on preventing it forever. My personal view is that if the foreigners construct lines on their own in Treaty Port areas without reporting to the local authorities, the prohibition may not be effective. Perhaps Chinese will also imitate the foreign technologies, and start to put up wires themselves. They could change the language from English to Chinese and the script from the English [alphabet] to Chinese characters and study [the technology] until they are quite familiar with it. News could be disseminated from afar, and much faster compared with

sending letters by official courier. By then we have reached the time we cannot prohibit it at all. The only approach left would be that we ourselves establish [the telegraph] lines in order to compete with their lines. Nevertheless, ignoring these issues for the present, I shall continue to find a way to prohibit [telegraphs]. And [I will] definitely not show the least hesitation![4]

As Li had predicted, in 1888 foreigners did surreptitiously build telegraph networks, the first of these networks built in the Chinese territories under foreign control. As the nineteenth century closed, the Chinese government itself began to build networks, particularly as a defense against Japan's growing military power.[5]

In contrast, in other economies, history shaped very different attitudes toward the government's role in telecommunications development. In the United States in 1893 and 1894, Alexander Graham Bell's key patents expired, thus allowing a number of companies to enter the market and compete fiercely for subscribers, making this one of the rapid periods of growth in U.S. telecommunications history. However, Bell's company, American Telephone & Telegraph (AT&T), began purchasing many of its competitors, including the country's largest telegraph company, Western Union, creating an effective monopoly. The response of the United States government to the telephone as a new technology was to focus on preventing anticompetitive behavior. This remained the central framework for the relationship between government and operator in the United States until 1984, when AT&T was broken into several regional companies and a long distance company.[6]

In Europe, some governments took an approach similar to that of the Americans, whereas others opted to establish state-owned monopolies. In the early twentieth century, one observer noted that in every Scandinavian community, it seemed imperative to have "a church, a school, [and] a telephone exchange." In Sweden, Denmark, and Norway, the governments permitted a number of companies to build telephone networks and provide service.

In contrast, in Germany, Great Britain, and France, the governments protected their state-owned telegraph monopolies and slowed telephone service deployment.[7] By 1914, about 10 percent of people in the Nordic cities had telephones, compared with less than 2 percent of urban citizens in France, Great Britain, and Germany. Not until the

1960s, when technology improved and there was public demand for better service and modern equipment, did both Great Britain and France make telecommunications development a higher priority, increase the telecommunications monopoly's access to capital, and enable greater investment.[8]

In late nineteenth-century Japan, under the Meiji government, a central concern was the establishment of the requisite technical knowledge and skill to manage the telecommunications services and to manufacture telecommunications equipment without relying on foreign companies. The government invested in technology industries, including telecommunications. Some of the firms from that era became today's giants, such as Toshiba and Nippon Electronic Company (NEC). By 1888, just over ten years after the telephone was invented, the government had a network built with Japanese-manufactured equipment to link its offices. In 1889, the government established a government monopoly to provide telecommunications services, the basic model for the industry for about fifty years. After the devastation of World War II, the government turned to the Nippon Telephone and Telegraph (NTT) monopoly to rebuild. For decades, this policy to promote industry has colored Japan's telecommunications policy, and it explains the historical weakness of the Ministry of Post and Telecommunications in directing telecommunications policy in Japan.[9] Today that ministry has been transformed into the Ministry of Information and Communications, and the increase in number of competitors in the market has strengthened its hand.

Historical conditions influence the posture that regulators take toward their markets today. Americans are relatively speaking much more concerned about anticompetitive behavior and tend to look for innovation from small upstarts. Some European regulators and the Japanese rely heavily on their incumbents to innovate and develop their national markets and, to some extent, are willing to protect them from excessive rivalry. In China, the impact of history is also apparent.

Disruption and Stagnation: China's First 100 Years with the Telephone

In 1882, six years after the telephone was invented, telephone service began in China. Initially, it was operated only by foreigners and was available only in the foreign concession areas of Shanghai. The Chinese government allowed investment and operation of privately owned telecommunications services as long as they were under official government supervision. Within this framework, local telephone services developed in major cities, such as Beijing, Tianjin, and Nanjing. Some networks were government projects, such as the Tianjin–Shanghai cable, which was paid for by prominent modernizer Li Hongzhang with funds borrowed from the military payroll budget. A Danish concern, the Great Northern Telegraph Company, built a cable between Shanghai and Beijing in 1900. After four years the Chinese government demanded control and eventually purchased the link. In 1901, the government conceptually approved the creation of the Ministry of Post and Telecommunications.[10] Yuan Shikai, minister for telecommunications in 1905, reported:

> Recently, foreign businessmen have set up unauthorized telephone facilities in concession areas in the open port cities, making these facilities a *fait accompli*. Furthermore, they have even extended their lines to the inland to reap our profit. This is too much. I hereby suggest to your Majesty to declare that all telephone facilities in China should be administered by the Directorate General of Telegraph. Except for the existing telephone facilities in the open port cities, no telephone facility by anybody anywhere is permitted unless it is authorized by the Directorate General of Telegraph. This is for the purpose of protecting our profit in telecommunications and national sovereignty.[11]

Six years after the government gave its approval, the Ministry for Post and Telecommunications was finally established in 1907. The following year the ministry nationalized all telecommunications services, buying the commercial operators and taking over provincial services.[12]

When the Qing dynasty fell in 1911, the successor Republican government did not have a centralized approach toward telecommunications development. Various ministries vied for investment funds, often in the form of loans from foreign companies interested in furthering their presence in the market. As a result, the Ministry of Transportation, the army, and the navy all independently funded and developed their own networks, a pattern that would persist in Communist China after 1949. When the Nationalist government took power in 1928, it renewed the Qing's efforts to nationalize communications networks.

The Nationalist government established a network of international relay stations, to compete with the foreign-owned monopoly on international telecommunications. Then it notified the companies that their contracts for international services would not be renewed and began negotiations with them to take control of the physical network.[13] However, the Sino-Japanese War and the subsequent Chinese Civil War destroyed much of the network. Subscribership fell from 50,000 in 1936 to 8,000 in 1944. In those same years, long distance lines fell from 52,000 to 4,000 kilometers.[14]

Established in 1949, the People's Republic of China did not consider the telecommunications sector a high priority industry for its first thirty years of existence and invested little in the network. The Ministry of Telecommunications was reestablished in 1950 and operated the network until the Great Leap Forward interrupted it later that decade. The Great Leap Forward was a campaign by Mao Zedong to accelerate economic development by sheer will power alone, without the benefit of capital or technology, which in the long run was economically destructive. The Great Leap Forward was soon followed by the Cultural Revolution in the 1960s, Mao's great ideological movement to achieve continuous revolution. Elites of all kinds were subject to political attack. Much of the economy suffered, the telecom infrastructure included. During the late 1960s, the telecom ministry lost control over the network to the military. The ministry itself was dissolved in 1969, and control over the network was relegated to the provincial authorities. Meanwhile, in other parts of the world, the 1960s were a time of rapid technological innovation in telecommunications.

The Ministry of Posts and Telecommunications (MPT) was reestablished in 1973. After the Cultural Revolution, politics stabilized and the economy began to make progress. However, there had been little investment in telecommunications, and the infrastructure in place was not able to meet demand. Beginning in 1976, ministries other than the MPT were allowed to build telecommunications networks in order to meet their own internal needs, as had occurred in the Republican period of the early twentieth century.

The first 100 years of the telephone in China consisted of short cycles of government centralization over the network, followed by resistance and decentralization of control, and then by renewed efforts at centralization. In the late nineteenth century, the Qing government focused on asserting control over private and foreign-owned networks. The Nationalist government sought not only to gain control of foreign-owned networks but also to establish authority over provincial networks. A series of political and economic shocks, beginning in the late nineteenth century and extending through the 1960s, rarely gave the sector long enough respite to develop. Lack of investment also stunted growth.

Rapid Growth in Telecommunications Service: 1980s Forward

In the late 1970s, the Chinese government made economic reforms a priority, the economy grew, and demand for telecommunications services outstripped supply. In 1979, the MPT centralized its authority over the network. In 1980, in an effort to increase the funds available for telecommunications investment, the MPT, the Ministry of Finance, and the State Price Administration established a nationwide schedule of installation fees for telephone service, ranging between 1000 and 2000 yuan (US$120–$240). As reforms deepened, telecommunications development became a more important priority for the government. The government gave the telecommunications industry preferential tax rates, privileged rights to retain foreign exchange, and easier terms on repayment of state loans. The 1980s were also an era in which four special economic zones and fourteen coastal cities were permitted to experiment with market economy measures. By 1991, these areas accounted for nearly a quarter of the telecommunications network in China.[15]

Also during this period, in 1982, the State Council and the Central Military Commission issued its first set of rules for the telecommunications industry, the Regulations on the Protection of Telecommunications Lines. These rules defined telecommunications lines and provided for sanction against those who might damage them. Although some aspects of the Chinese economy grew more open to foreign participation, telecommunications was not among them. Between 1981 and 2007, at least a half dozen statements by the State Council and the MPT affirmed that foreigners were prohibited from management or investment in telecommunications.[16]

The 1990s were a period of rapid telecommunications growth in China, as Figure 2.1 demonstrates. Notably, cellular phones using

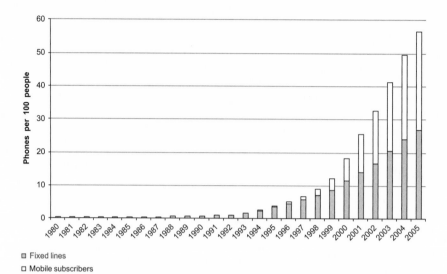

□ Fixed lines
□ Mobile subscribers

FIGURE 2.1 China: Phones per 100 people, 1980–2005
SOURCE: International Telecommunications Union

wireless telephony technology emerged during this decade as a major commercial service. In areas dense with customers, wireless networks were often cheaper and quicker to install than wireline networks. By 2001, nearly half of all telephone service subscriptions were for wireless service.

Although the numbers in Figure 2.1 may appear to indicate that on average telecommunications service still is not widely available in China, actually there is great disparity among different regions. In urban areas, telecommunications service is virtually everywhere, but in some rural areas, it is nearly nonexistent. Figures 2.2 and 2.3 show how telephone service availability ranges from thirty-five mainlines per 100 people in Shanghai to fewer than five in Guizhou province in western China. Similarly, cellular subscription rates range from over twenty-five per 100 in Beijing to two in Guizhou.

The current literature in telecommunications suggests that telecommunications services begin to contribute significantly to overall economic development when phones are available to forty or more people per 100.[17] Major cities in China already approach this level of

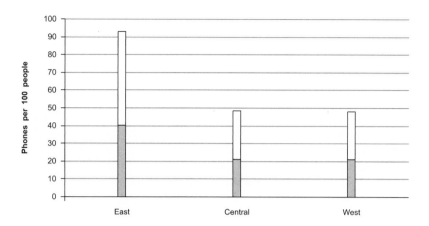

FIGURE 2.2 China by region: Total phones per 100 people, December 2006
SOURCE: Ministry of Information Industry

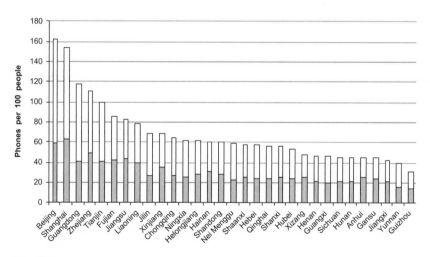

FIGURE 2.3 China by province: Total phones per 100 people, December 2006
SOURCE: Ministry of Information Industry

development. A major challenge to China, therefore, is how to make telecommunications service available to residents in rural areas and in the economically less developed regions of central and western China.

China Today Compared with Other Countries: Better Than Most, Behind Some Others

Telecommunications growth in China places it well ahead of other large developing countries, most especially compared with those of South Asia. However, compared with leading industrialized countries, including its East Asian neighbors, China still lags behind. For China, its position is a source of pride in its achievements mixed with a sense of urgent need to catch up with the latest global developments.

Figure 2.4 compares several countries with populations greater than 100 million. In the past two decades, China has broken away from

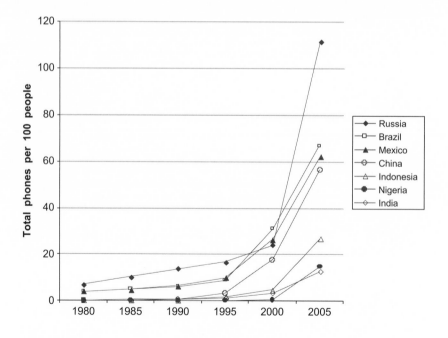

FIGURE 2.4 China and large emerging economies: Total phones per 100 people, 1980–2005
SOURCE: International Telecommunications Union

those large developing countries—Indonesia, India, Pakistan, Nigeria, and Bangladesh—where telephone subscribership persists below 10–15 percent of the population. It has joined the ranks of middle-income countries like Brazil, Mexico, and Russia.

Compared with the world's leading economies, however, China's telecommunications development falls far short. France, Germany, Japan, the United Kingdom, and the United States have made telecommunications an investment priority, and in combination with technical advances, there has been a massive growth in services in these countries (see Figure 2.5). China's level of telecommunications development as of 2002 was reached by most of these countries in 1975 and before 1960 in the United States.

An intermediate comparison is to look at some of China's geographic neighbors that have succeeded in wide deployment of a telecommunications network (see Figure 2.6). By 1995, there were over

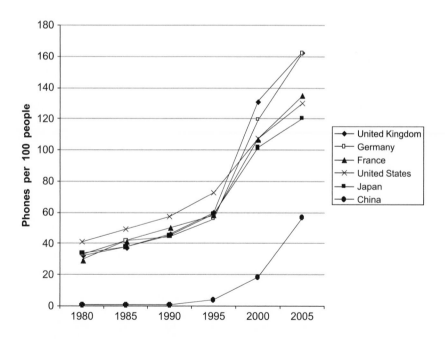

FIGURE 2.5 China and high income countries: Total phones per 100 people, 1980–2005
SOURCE: International Telecommunications Union

twelve cellular subscribers per 100 people in Hong Kong. By 2000, wireless subscriptions per 100 exceed mainlines per 100 in all of these markets except China.

In the markets of China's neighbors, the key factors to rapid telecommunications development were policy and regulatory decisions to allow competition, which created a climate salutary for investment. These economies took common steps in the liberalization of a telecommunications market: they separated the regulatory authority from the operator of telecommunications services and introduced competition in cellular service, domestic long and local service, and international long distance service. As of 2002, China had passed all the major milestones to telecommunications liberalization, a success that is reflected in the high availability of telecommunications services for a country at its economic development level. Where China differs, however, is in the degree of competition allowed in these various market segments and in its barriers against foreign investment.

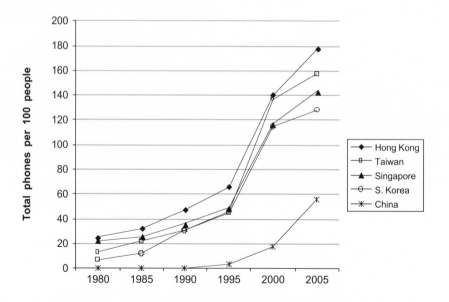

FIGURE 2.6 China and Asia neighbors: Total phones per 100 people, 1980–2005
SOURCE: International Telecommunications Union

Conclusion

A sense of pride and confidence from recent achievement tempered by an urgent quest to improve the country's international stature and a wariness of foreigners consumes China's telecommunications policy. As in other countries, the history of China's telecommunications development has shaped in part its current policy approaches. Although China had limited service shortly after the telephone was invented, the service was part of the wave of foreign technologies and ideas that the Qing Dynasty government of the time went to great lengths to isolate and contain. Although other countries took a similarly nationalistic view and established state control over telecommunications, China's resistance combined with decades of international and domestic war and turmoil delayed the development of any significant telecommunications network before the 1980s. Suspicion of foreign operators and their technology borne from this period is still reflected in current policies that limit new entry into the market and support the state's ability to monitor information flow over the telecommunications networks. The economic reforms of the Deng Xiaoping era created changes that improved telecommunications investment in China, and vast growth occurred in the 1980s and particularly in the 1990s. Compared with other large developing countries, China's growth has been spectacular and is a source of national pride and government confidence. However, compared with other markets, such as its industrialized neighbors Hong Kong, Taiwan, Korea, and Singapore, which have taken advantage of advances in competition theory and new technologies such as cellular phones, China is still in the midst of fundamental transitions. Thus follows China's sense of urgency to keep up with global developments. These feelings of insecurity, pride, and confidence mixed with urgency have shaped the main debates on telecommunications policy in China today.

3   Evolution of the Telecommunications Policymaker

Bargaining Among Interests

Why is a regulator necessary? In a ball game, when there is only one team on the field, there is not much of a game and certainly not much need for a referee. The instant a second team appears, however, it matters very much whether there is a referee. And furthermore, any bias the referee might have can change the game's final outcome. The telecommunications market in China, and other countries, in this respect is similar to such a ball game. In the days of a monopoly, there is no need for a regulator. Once there is a second, third, or more operators, the game works only if there is a good regulator.

In the case of China, from the beginning there was no separation between the monopoly operation and oversight—it was all in one entity, the MPT. However, once China introduced Unicom, the second team, into the market, the absence of a regulator-referee meant that the game was stacked in favor of the veteran. No new entrant would have a fair chance. Furthermore, starting around 2000, new technologies emerged that enable cable television networks to offer services comparable to those of telecommunications networks. It was as if there were not only baseball teams but also basketball teams on the same playing field. Cable networks, which historically have their own sets of rules and regulators, began competing with the telecommunications institutions, which were just newly established.

In the 1980s, as a result of the growing economy, demand for telecommunications services rose dramatically. To fulfill this demand, in 1988 China had to restructure the telecommunications industry. There was an economy-wide effort to separate government oversight functions from business operations, but in telecommunications that separation took place only within MPT. However, while other sectors separated oversight from business functions, telecommunications was exempted from this division partially because it was considered a sensitive national infrastructure. MPT retained both oversight and operations responsibility for wireline and wireless telecommunications services. In 1988, only within MPT was there a specialization of offices. The policymaking and regulation offices, such as Telecommunications Administration, Policy and Regulation, Science and Technology, and Finance, were separated internally from the Directorate General of Telecommunications (DGT), which ran the network.[1] Despite this reorganization, MPT continued to make policy decisions that favored the DGT monopoly. These decisions included minimizing entry of competition into the market and trying to boost wholesale and retail rates, both of which will be discussed in subsequent chapters. The monopoly's efforts were still inadequate to meet public demand for services (see Figure 3.1), which led to other government entities seeking opportunities to enter into the market themselves.

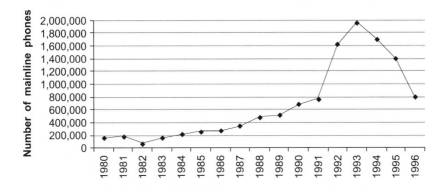

FIGURE 3.1 Waiting list for mainline phones
SOURCE: International Telecommunications Union

In 1993, as the official waiting list for mainline phones skyrocketed to two million, the State Council intervened in telecommunications
policy and issued regulations allowing other Chinese companies to provide value-added telecommunications services, such as paging services.[2]
The Ministry of Electronic Industry (MEI), primarily responsible for the
manufacture of electronic equipment, led a coalition of ministries to
back a new telecommunications operator—Unicom. In the early 1990s,
MPT had entered into joint ventures with foreign companies to produce
telecommunications equipment, invading MEI's turf and creating an
incentive for MEI to enter MPT's industry sector.[3]

In 1994, the State Council agreed to a joint proposal from several
influential ministries for the deregulation of the Chinese telecommunications market.[4] Unicom was licensed, a move backed by MEI and others, including the Ministry of Railways. The same year, state-owned
enterprise Jitong was licensed to provide value-added services. The People's Liberation Army offered commercial wireless services—both cellular phone service and paging—at this time as well.[5] The need for a fair
regulator-referee thus became urgent.

Evolving International Norms: Developments in Neighboring Countries

While China was in the midst of these changes, an international
consensus was forming that like referees, regulators should be independent of political pressure from other parts of the government, of commercial pressure from the regulated companies, and of populist consumer
pressure.[6] Of the three possible pressures that are typically exerted on a
regulatory agency—political, commercial, and consumer—political and
commercial interests are concentrated in few hands, whereas consumer
interests tend to be widely dispersed. Consequently, as a practical matter
in most countries, political or commercial interests, not consumer interests, most easily capture the regulator. The United States, United Kingdom, and Japan, three markets that were early leaders in introducing
competition in telecommunications, offer contrasting experiences on the
establishment of a regulatory body separate from the network operator.

Of the regulatory bodies in these three countries, the FCC has the
most formal shields against influence from politicians and its regulated

TABLE 3.1   Approaches to regulatory organization in three leading
competitive markets

	Regulator relationship with ministry	Regulator relationship with incumbent operator	Competition begins
United States	Completely separate	None, never government owned	Long distance, 1982
United Kingdom	Regulator advises ministry	None, privatized in 1984	Duopoly, 1982, Liberalization, 1990
Japan	Ministry is regulator	Government owns operator, privatization in process	Long distance, 1985

companies (see Table 3.1). In the United States, the major telecommunications networks have always been privately owned. The commissioners of the FCC, though nominated by the U.S. president, report to the U.S. Congress. Further, the commissioners cannot be removed by either the executive or legislative branches, should they be unhappy with FCC decisions.

In the United Kingdom, the government separated telecommunications operator British Telecommunications (BT) from the government's postal office in 1981 and privatized BT in 1984. The regulator, the Office of Telecommunications (Oftel), advises the relevant ministry but has an independently appointed leader, the Director General of Telecommunications.[7] In 2003, the United Kingdom merged its telecom, broadcast, and other related organizations into a single regulatory authority of communications, the Office of Communications (Ofcom). The regulator is free of conflict of interest inherent in owning an operator. Although the regulator has a reputation for independence, its major decisions often remain in the form of recommendations to the Department of Trade and Industry, whose minister serves the prime minister's government. The British approach has been influential in its former colonies throughout Asia and the Americas.

In Japan after World War II, the Ministry of Communications provided telecommunications services. In 1952, NTT was established as a state-owned company to provide telecommunications services separate from Japan's Ministry of Posts and Telecommunications (MPT), the policymaker and regulator. MPT was absorbed into the Ministry of Public Management, Home Affairs, Posts, and Telecommunications (MPHPT), recently renamed the Ministry of Internal Affairs and Communications, and continues to be both policymaker and regulator. Its leader is a cabinet minister, whom the prime minister appoints and can remove. In Japan, therefore, there is little formal separation between regulatory and political decisions and between the interests of the government as operator and overseer of the industry. However, the customary absence of a revolving door between industry and government, except at the most senior levels of the Japanese bureaucracy, does create an informal separation of these interests. The Japanese approach has been particularly influential in Asia.

While China was debating how to organize its regulatory structure, the significance of independent regulators grew in other countries, especially in the Asia regional neighborhood. In Hong Kong, the telecommunications operator had always been private and, therefore, separate from the government. In 1992, the Telecommunications Authority of Singapore was separated from the government-owned operator Singapore Telecom. In 1993, Hong Kong's Office of the Telecommunications Authority was established as an entity separate from the postal services office, which affirmed the government's interest in creating a strong regulator. In 1994, Korea established the Ministry of Information and Communications as separate from operator Korea Telecom. In 1996, Taiwan separated the policymaker Directorate General of Telecommunications from operator Chunghwa Telecom.

In 1997, the WTO's Basic Telecommunications Agreement was reached, and members' commitments went into effect beginning in 1998. Part of the agreement was a "reference paper" containing regulatory principles to which members would adhere. These included principles of interconnection, licensing, and universal service. However, of particular interest to the discussion of regulatory organizations, the reference paper also enshrined the principle of an independent regulator. The fifth principle states, "Independent regulators: The regulatory body is separate from, and not accountable to, any supplier of basic telecommunications services. The decisions of and the procedures used by regulators shall be impartial with respect to all market participants."

China, in the midst of WTO membership accession negotiations at the time, was aware of the reference paper and the widespread support for it in the international telecommunications community. In tandem with the WTO discussions, the International Telecommunications Union (ITU) launched a series of study sessions on the "establishment of an independent regulatory body," which concluded in 2001 that such bodies should be "separate from interested commercial parties," with the caveat that "the jurisdiction and mandate of an independent telecommunications regulatory body depends largely on its relationship with the other entities in the telecommunications sector, such as government ministries, competition authorities and the telecommunications operators themselves."[8] More aggressively, the regional grouping Asia Pacific Economic Cooperation (APEC) organization's Telecommunications and Information Working Group created a WTO Task Group, chaired by Taiwan. Moving faster than the ITU, it released a 2001 report that assumed that regulatory agencies would be separate from network operators and focused instead on whether the regulator was separate from the policymaking authority. Of the twenty-one member economies, thirteen had regulatory authorities that were separate from policymakers. Nine of the authorities were established after 1990.[9]

China Separates Ministry from Operator

While these discussions and changes were underway internationally, China's duopoly competition failed to take root, in large measure due to the absence of a fair regulator-referee. In 1995, Unicom began offering wireless services in the major cities of Guangzhou, Shanghai, Beijing, and Tianjin and investing in wireline operations in Tianjin.[10] MPT's decisions, however, continued to favor its affiliated operating arm, China Telecommunications, in disputes with China Unicom. The conflict between the carriers remained unresolved for years, sharply curtailing Unicom's growth. Despite its general license to provide all telecommunications services nationwide, Unicom was geographically constrained to a handful of cities and then mostly could offer only mobile services.[11] Unicom's problems centered around China Telecom's refusal to offer interconnection on reasonable terms, a technical problem that will be discussed further in Chapter 6. Interconnection service would enable Unicom's customers to call the customers of China Telecom. As Unicom was small and China Telecommunications was large, interconnection was indispensable for Unicom but unessential for China Telecom.

MPT's failure to manage in a timely and reasonable manner the disputes between China Telecommunications and Unicom led to further intervention by the State Council and eventually to rounds of proposals on how to reorganize the ministry. In 1997, the State Council proposed an "informatization plan," which would sever the relationship between the MPT and China Telecom. The plan reportedly was blocked by MPT Minister Wu Jichuan until a version that guaranteed the preservation of MPT jobs emerged. This proposal was to merge the MPT and the MEI, the patron ministry of Unicom.[12]

With the backdrop of its rapidly developing neighbors establishing regulators separate from their operators and the ever present discussion of independent regulation in international and regional telecommunications organizations, the Chinese government proceeded with key decisions in 1998. The Ministry of Information Industry (MII) was formed in 1998. Essentially, it appeared to be a conservative transformation, which organized the new MII around the old MPT. MII would be separate from China Telecom; this was an organizational split that not only took place at Beijing headquarters but also was replicated at the provincial telecommunications administration level. The divestiture of regulatory and operational activities was scheduled to occur at national and provincial levels in 2000, although practically, this was completed only in 2002. This reorganization of the industry and regulator involved 1.2 million workers.[13]

Even though the story of individual leaders is not a sufficient explanation for policy changes in China, the politicking surrounding the leadership of the new MII does offer some insight into the dynamics at play in the telecommunications arena. In the days leading up to the MII's formation, MEI Vice Minister Liu Jianfeng's name appeared several times in the media as likely to succeed Minister Wu.[14] However, on March 31, 1998, when the leadership of the new MII was announced, Wu Jichuan was named minister; he was one of only six ministers who survived that year's reshuffling of ministerial responsibilities. Also named with him were five vice ministers: two former MPT vice ministers and three former MEI vice ministers. The State Council Informatization

Leading Group Office, a nebulous, potentially rivalrous intermediary organization between the old MPT and the State Council leadership, was abolished and taken over by MII. The Leading Group's leader, Zou Jiahua, retired, and his portfolio was assumed by new Vice Premier Wu Bangguo.[15]

There is little empirical evidence to document why these individual job assignments occurred. However, observers offer their own explanations. Wu began service at MPT in 1964 and is strongly identified with the strategy of telecommunications development through a government-controlled monopoly, a successful strategy through most of the 1990s. His appointment as MII minister was a victory for this policy. The reappointment of an MEI official, the patron ministry of competitor Unicom, would have been interpreted as a victory for those pushing for greater competition.[16] Finally, although the status of leading groups in the State Council is somewhat obscure, the existence of such groups usually somewhat lessens the importance of those ministries who must be guided by them. The abolition of the State Council Informatization Leading Group Office could be construed as an affirmation of MII as the leading organ responsible for telecommunications policy, free of the possible interference that a State Council group's existence might imply, said one Chinese observer.[17] An alternative, and not necessarily contradictory, explanation for Wu's survival is that he was the only minister remaining in government who had been appointed originally by Li Peng, Zhu Rongji's predecessor as premier. Observers opined that President Jiang Zemin had been reluctant to sweep out all of Li Peng's supporters and that, therefore, Wu remained with MII.[18]

In 1999, former MPT Senior Vice Minister Yang Xianzhu became chairman and president of Unicom, a personnel action interpreted by the market as a concrete demonstration that MEI's patronage of China Unicom was transferred to the newly established MII. Improved interconnection with China Telecommunications led to a rapid increase in subscribership. The improvements included expanded scope, quicker procedures, lower costs, and improved technical specifications. Unicom's scope for service previously was limited to mobile services, but with changes in the interconnection agreements, China Telecommunications no longer required Unicom to use China Telecom's network to provide international services. Unicom could build and operate its own international network. As a result of these changes in the interconnection framework, the quality of service Unicom provided to its subscribers improved. Between 1998 and 1999, China Unicom's subscribership tripled from 1.4 million to 5.2 million.[19] However, although Unicom reportedly welcomed the reorganization of MPT into MII, there were still complaints about MII's failure to fully incorporate the former MEI and about continued favoritism for China Telecom.[20]

Although some issues were resolved by the creation of MII, others remained open. Most problematic for the future was authority over telecommunications types of services, including the Internet, which passed over networks overseen by the broadcasting authority. Returning to the analogy that opened the chapter, this was the equivalent of having basketball teams on the field in the midst of a baseball game. It had been proposed that some of the responsibilities belonging to the Ministry of Radio, Film, and Television (MRFT), such as oversight over cable networks, be transferred to the new MII. The MRFT's regulation of content and propaganda would be transferred to the Ministry of Culture, according to this proposal.[21] However, subsequent practical events demonstrated that although in principle telecom carriers should be able to enter the television market, in practice they could not because of the opposition of the MRFT, which survived a sweeping government administrative reform as a lower ranking agency—SARFT.[22] SARFT retained operational control over the cable networks and the services provided over those networks. The resolution of the conflict between the regulation of networks and the regulation of content was thus deferred.

Convergence of Telecommunications and Broadcasting Systems: Clash of Economic and Ideological Concerns

How is it that basketball players (i.e., the broadcasters) had shown up on the baseball players' (i.e., the telecommunications operators') field? In the past, broadcasting was conventionally considered an activity whereby content was delivered from one point, such as a television station, to many points, such as everyone's television sets. The conventional view of telecommunications was of point-to-point transmission—for example, a conversation that traveled from my telephone handset to yours. Technical advances, also associated with the development of the

Internet, meant that one-to-many communications could occur over telephone lines—think of an e-mail broadcast from one computer to lots of other people. Also, some one-to-one communications, such as telephone calls and e-mail from one person to another, could be transported over the cable network.

Cable television networks historically have arisen in many countries as a means of providing a clearer signal to viewers of over-the-air, also known as terrestrial, broadcasting. Over time, cable television operators have offered far more programming than simple rebroadcast of terrestrial channels. Technical innovations allowed the emergence of nonvideo programming services on cable networks, such as telephone service and Internet service. These became serious commercial services in the mid-1990s in countries that early adopted such innovations. In the United States, cable networks began offering cable modem service, an Internet access service that offered far higher speeds than dial-up service over the telephone line. Canada and Korea were also early adopters. In international telecommunications organizations, debates turned not only to the development of Internet access but also to the development of broadband Internet service, which offered users quicker access to greater volumes of content on the Internet. In the first decade of the twenty-first century, the two primary technologies used by households for broadband service were cable modem service and digital subscriber line (DSL), a technology that uses a wireline telephone line.

International policy discussions related to broadband Internet began in earnest in 2001. A year later, the Organisation for Economic Co-operation and Development (OECD) released a landmark study of broadband Internet service, which they defined as 128 kbps, twice the speed of dial-up Internet service, that demonstrated the key catalytic role of cable networks in Internet growth.[23] This was a harbinger of a shift in international communications debates away from a narrow focus on telecommunications networks to a broader consideration of the importance of other communications networks, including cable television networks. This international discussion was reflected in China as well.[24]

As in many other countries, cable television in China developed locally as an effort to bring better terrestrial television signals and expanded programming to communities. Peculiar to China and some other authoritarian states, the government funds cable network investment and subsidizes services not only to generate revenue, but also as an essential element of its propaganda apparatus. Large-scale growth of public cable television networks began in the 1980s because of government concern about the perceived ideological threat posed by foreign satellite television. To this day, the Communist Party's Propaganda Department subsidizes basic cable rates and influences programming on cable networks. In urban areas, cable television is offered inexpensively and has far more subscribers than satellite television, a network that enables easy distribution of foreign content. Rural areas, in contrast, have less access to terrestrial and cable television and rely more on satellite service.[25]

Today, SARFT is responsible for radio and television programming, particularly foreign content, and controls access to satellite and cable channels. Its Beijing headquarters are closely linked to the Chinese Communist Party propaganda offices, and similar links are replicated at the provincial and local levels of government. It is primarily the local offices that undertake the practical operation of the cable television networks. In 1997, there were 50 million cable television subscribers. By 1998, there were 60 million; by 1999, 70 million; by 2006, 126 million. These subscribers receive service from a scattered collection of 1,200 cable television stations, each managed and financed autonomously by local government offices, the local SARFT branch, and the local Communist Party office.[26]

SARFT has been trying for some time to consolidate the cable television industry. For example, in early 2002, there were ten different cable operations in the Beijing area that were now undergoing consolidation.[27] Consolidating the cable network eases the offering of television and other services, such as Internet and telephony.[28] However, consolidation faces obstacles. Ownership of the many operations is scattered among regional local and municipal governments; they offer different services and are in different financial condition.

Today, Internet access is offered over some cable networks, although it is not clear whether SARFT or MII has responsibility for regulating these services. The opportunity to offer telephony over cable networks directly threatens the wireline telecommunications monopoly in China. Conversations with local SARFT officials suggest that the official line is that such services, although technically possible, are not offered for policy reasons. However, other officials noted that such services have been available over cable networks in Shanghai.[29] These conflicting reports suggest that cable networks continue to be wary of offering Internet and telephony services but that experimentation exists in certain localities.

In 1997, the State Council decreed that MRFT, SARFT's predecessor, could build a nationwide cable network and that it could use MPT's infrastructure to do so. MPT opposed this decision, and cable television in China remains today a largely locally developed phenomenon. But MRFT would continue to try to invest and expand further its cable network and increase the variety and value of services these networks could offer the public. The fierce rivalry between China Telecommunications and SARFT was heightened by China's accession to the WTO and by the commitments to foreign participation in telecommunications that this accession entailed. SARFT still seeks to consolidate current cable networks and to continue expanding while at the same time keeping out other ministries. China's WTO commitments allow foreign companies to participate in limited sections of the telecommunications market. SARFT cites these foreign participation commitments as a reason for keeping telecommunications companies out of the cable television market. Foreign investment in cable services, it asserts, would present a national security risk.[30]

According to media reports, when MII was reorganized in 1998, it was supposed to have regulatory power over all public broadcasting networks, including cable, although SARFT would retain operations of the cable networks. MII had lost all operational control over the telecommunications networks, but SARFT retained operational control over broadcasting, primarily because of the importance of these networks to the Communist Party's propaganda network.[31] However, as MII tried to assert regulatory power over broadcasting by stating that new laws would allow broadcasters to provide telecommunications services and vice versa, its tenuous authority over the broadcasting networks became apparent. In July 2000, Zhang Chunjiang, vice minister of MII, remarked that the domestic telecommunications and cable television operators should be able to enter each others' markets to promote competition. Shortly thereafter, a SARFT official accepted the notion that cable operators could offer telecommunication services but stated that the organization was unlikely to open the cable television sector to telecommunications companies. In 2001, an MII official Hua Xia reiterated that same point: "we always advocate granting cable television networks access to the telecommunications market and giving state-owned telecommunications companies access to the cable television market to realize mutual access." Hua further clarified this point by noting that this integration does not involve production of content and that foreign businesses would not have access to cable television markets, consistent with the government's policy that foreign content would threaten social stability.[32] However, SARFT again demurred, stating that it is interested in using the cable networks for telephony and Internet access as a competitor to China Telecommunications but cannot do so under the existing law. SARFT is also believed to be resisting MII's efforts to consolidate its authority through a new telecommunications law.[33]

In addition to the divergent interpretations of law and jurisdiction, there have been physical scuffles between these two entities. In 1997, a riot occurred in Zhuzhou, Hunan, between the supporters of the local Post and Telecommunications Administration and the local Radio, Film, and Television office because the latter had begun offering telephony services over its cable networks. In March 1999, MII announced that IP telephony could only be offered by certain licensed operators—China Telecom, China Unicom, and Jitong—partly because a number of cable operators, among other enterprises, had begun experimenting with the technology. In 1999, an operator in Shandong province began offering cable telephony. Around the same time, the Qingdao cable television network, with 750,000 subscribers, began offering Internet access. MII has reportedly tried to block broadcasters' access to international Internet gateways, but some cable television stations were able to use the international gateway of Jitong, a state-owned enterprise rival to China Telecom in data services.[34]

In May 1999, Netcom, in an effort coordinated by SARFT, the Ministry of Railways, and the Shanghai municipal government, received approval to provide telecommunications service. Netcom was licensed to compete against China Telecommunications and Unicom. It had permission to establish an IP telecommunications network to provide cable television services, IP telephony, and Internet access. China Netcom was said to be backed by Jiang Mianheng, son of Jiang Zemin, the country's president at the time.[35]

The possibility of providing television over the Internet has now opened a new jurisdictional area over which to fight. SARFT has succeeded in requiring telephone companies to work with commercial broadcasters if they want to offer IPTV services, but gray areas still exist. In 2006, Baidu.com partnered with MTV, owned by Viacom, one of the largest media companies in the United States, to provide music videos over its website. Baidu stated that there was no need for its offerings to have government approval, as they were no different than other audiovisual content on the Internet, but SARFT publicly indicated that it was beginning a review of the case. The Five-Year Plans of SARFT and MII, released in 2007, both emphasize the importance of their industry to national security; SARFT note its interest in bringing in more foreign culture, as long as it is not harmful to China.[36]

Emergence of Other Government Players in the Industry

SARFT's success in obtaining approval for Netcom to enter the market in 1999 reflected the government's continuing frustration with MII and the performance of the telecommunications market. Although telecommunications was growing very rapidly, it still was not meeting the demands of the market, as reflected by popular consumer complaints. Media reports at the time observed that consumer complaints about the high service charges and poor quality of China Telecom's service had grown, and that consumers blamed its monopoly status as a source of these problems. One Kyodo news report noted:

> One of the greatest grievances is the [China Telecom's] long-standing custom of charging for a three-minute call even if it only lasted for 10 seconds. Even worse, though, is the habit of considering a call "connected" after a certain number of rings—when, in fact, there was no answer . . . Dozens of lawsuits have been filed by consumers across the country claiming telecommunications operators charge unreasonable fees for such items as line installation and extra charges for basic mobile communications services.[37]

The growth of consumer complaints forced the State Development Planning Commission (SDPC) to hold a hearing on telecommunications prices in late 1998, which will be discussed in detail in Chapter 7 case study five, on retail pricing. The SDPC then asked MII to overhaul its pricing policy for several services in early 1999.[38] Although the question of governmental organization around telecommunications was settled for the time being, continuing problems in the sector led the State Council to push for a reorganization of the industry.

Consequently, in December 1999, the State Council reestablished a "leading group for national information work." Chaired by Premier Zhu Rongji, this leading group had authority over information issues, including the Internet.[39] MII Minister Wu was a member of the group but was not appointed to a leadership position in it. Other members included Hu Jintao, president from 2003; Ding Guanggen, Chinese Communist Party's propaganda chief; and Zeng Peiyuan, a leading economic policymaker. The MII stated that although it had been organized to be the sole authority, other ministries had refused to relinquish control over their networks, making the State Council authority a necessity.[40]

Widely seen as a counterbalance to MII, the State Council Informatization Office supports the Leading Group. The office comprises a kind of executive body for the leading group and has about twenty staff. The office's broad mandate covers basic telecom, informatization projects, and network security for online transactions.[41] The new State Council Informatization Office first met in December 2001, chaired by then Premier Zhu Rongji. Some observers commented that the State Council Informatization Office might be a forerunner to an independent regulator—a kind of union between MII and SARFT to oversee the transition to broadband.[42] In a meeting with U.S. government officials in Washington DC, then head of the office Vice Minister Liu He stated that there was interest in China in the concept of independent regulatory organizations (*duli jianguan ji gou*) and that he believed that such "third party" objective regulation was relevant not only to telecommunications, but also in other areas, such as credit systems and standards. He demurred, however, on when such a regulator might be created.[43] At one level, some observers have said that the power of the State Council Informatization Office is weak compared with MII. Its small staff is no match for the larger and more expert MII bureaucracy. It lacks the specialized expertise necessary to engage in key technical debates. However, it appears to have played a key advisory role to the State Council leadership in the 2002 decision to split China Telecommunications into northern and southern companies, which will be discussed in detail in the next chapter.

In May 2003, another organ of the State Council was established, introducing yet another player into the debate over telecom reform. The State-owned Assets Supervision and Administration Commission (SASAC) was established to oversee all state-owned enterprises, not just those in the information industry.[44] The first example of SASAC interest in telecommunications emerged quickly. By the beginning of 2004, SASAC indicated it might consider yet another restructuring of the industry. Mobile operator Unicom appeared to be struggling, as compared with thriving operators China Telecom, Netcom, and China Mobile. The weaker operator might be split up among the stronger. Several years later, this proposal by SASAC persists unimplemented.[45] A second example of SASAC's role was the December 2006 announcement that the government would retain absolute control over several strategic industries: telecommunications, power, oil, petrochemicals, coal, civil aviation, and shipping. SASAC's announcement made clear that foreign investment would be prohibited or severely restricted in these sectors.[46]

The State Council's ability to reorganize the industry reflects not only its power in telecommunications policy relative to MII but also its power relative to the operators. All carriers are state-owned enterprises, and the State Council is the ultimate representative of the government's interest as owner of these companies. In areas as general as industry structure and as specific as interconnection policy, the State Council is the ultimate authority. These are areas where MII has been unable or unwilling to take major decisions without clear direction from the State Council. Although clear empirical documentation of such relationships is not available, from several interviews with close observers of these debates it can be surmised that observers' frustration with the State Council Informatization Office as a counterbalance to MII's favoritism for incumbent operators stems in part from the importance of detailed technical expertise in implementing telecommunications policy. Where that expertise is necessary, MII is able to maintain its positions, usually conservative ones that preserve the privileges of China Telecom. When larger policy questions are at stake, however, it must heed the direction of the State Council.

Conclusion

Institutional reform seems possible in China when there is a confluence of international consensus, differing domestic interests can be brokered, and market demands underscore the need for change. In the first cycle of reform in 1988, the government established a limited duopoly and recognized the value of separating oversight and policymaking from the commercial operations of the network. Internationally, the separation of policymaker from network operator has led to positive results for many states, but China stopped short of complete separation. In the second cycle of reform, international norms in telecommunications policy were codified in the WTO Basic Telecommunications Agreement. International discussions assumed that a separation of regulator and regulated was necessary and focused on whether regulatory agencies should be further insulated from direct political and commercial pressure by making them independent of policymaking institutions. In 1998, China concluded the separation of the operator China Telecommunications from the policymaker and established a new agency, the MII. However, in 1999 a new State Council Informatization Group was established, a sign in previous cycles that indicated a new restructuring of institutions might be under consideration. The establishment of SASAC to oversee all state-owned enterprises, including telecommunications operators, introduced into the field yet another powerful actor with the ability to influence the future of the industry.

Around 2000, international discussions began focusing on the practical questions related to the convergence of cable television and telecommunications networks. However, the convergence of these networks touches on questions of programming and content, which are the province of the Chinese Communist Party's Propaganda Department, a very powerful, ideological actor. Whether telecommunications interests will let the Propaganda Department's companies enter the telecommunications service market without similar concessions allowing telecommunications companies into broadcasting remains unclear. This tension holds back the China's telecommunications industry from straightforwardly taking advantage of the latest developments in telecommunications service technology, although in the provision of older forms of service—wireline and cellular telephony service and dial-up Internet service—there is still ample opportunity for growth. For the moment, although an international consensus has emerged, market demand for converged services in China is only beginning to gather momentum. Therefore, the conflicting domestic interests have not been settled sufficiently to pave the way for further regulatory evolution.

4   Running the Gauntlet
*Entry of New Firms into China's
Telecommunications Service Market*

Firms are not free to enter and exit China's telecommunications market. The government makes all decisions on whether an entity can provide commercial telecommunications service—even in cases where the communications network is already built—and the decisions are highly politicized and deeply affected by dynamics within the government's competing bureaucracies. No state-owned enterprise without the backing of at least one ministry has succeeded in gaining a license. At several important moments in liberalization, the MII has pointedly moved to protect China Telecom. These actions have been closely associated with former MII Minister Wu Jichuan. In counterpoint, at several key moments the State Council has demonstrated a determination to cut down China Telecom. At each decision of the State Council, former Premier Zhu Rongji was seen to lean against further protection of China Telecom.

Licensing in other countries is not always as politically fraught. At one extreme, in the United States, any firm that wishes to provide interstate telecommunications service need only register with the FCC; no application process is required. In Japan, although a more lengthy application is required, it is publicly available on the Internet, and hundreds of companies have licenses. Similarly, open licensing regimes exist in Hong Kong and Australia. China's license system is just the opposite of that found in a free and open market. Only enterprises backed by ministries have a remote chance of entry, and entry is no guarantee of fair treatment by either the regulator or the telecommunications incumbent.

Although in mature telecommunications markets the benefits of competition are unquestioned, whether competition is beneficial in developing telecommunications markets is still subject to debate.[1] One benefit of competition is that consumers can get more services, of greater variety and at diverse price levels. A second benefit is that competition disperses power among many buyers and sellers rather than concentrating these economic and political decisions in a few hands, whether government or private.[2] In the United States, the first concrete challenges to the idea that telecommunications was a natural monopoly occurred in the 1970s when competition was introduced in the production of telephones, once the exclusive purview of AT&T, which allowed such innovations as the fax machine to emerge. MCI contested AT&T's monopoly in the 1970s and became the first company to compete against AT&T in the long distance market. In the 1980s, AT&T was divested, and the long distance market was thrown open to any company that wished to enter.[3] Later, countries such as Japan, the United Kingdom, and Germany took similar approaches that became easier to implement as technology advances lowered the cost of building telecom networks. Furthermore, there have been several studies of developing countries that have shown that competition is important to developing a new national network, whether by jostling an inefficient incumbent into providing better service or by auctioning targeted subsidies to the lowest bidder.[4]

In international circles of the early 1990s, the benefits of competition in long distance and mobile services were well documented, and most industrialized countries were taking steps to implement such liberalization of their markets. For example, in late 1997, there were 700,000 people on the waiting list for cellular phones in Taiwan. That year, the government ended Chunghwa Telecom's monopoly on mobile telephone service by licensing several competing companies. At the end of 1997, four island-wide operators and two regional operators began offering cellular service to the public. Within five months, Chunghwa Telecom's share of the cellular phone market plunged from 100 percent to 40 percent. Between January 1998 and May 1999, a period of only a year and a half, cellular subscription in Taiwan rose from less than 10 percent to close to 35 percent of population. As a result, there occurred not only a major increase in subscriptions to cellular service but also a drop in the average call price by at least 10 percent, to NT$5 (US$0.25) per minute.[5]

It was in this international context that China began considering reform of its telecommunications policy. As documented in Chapter 3, general dissatisfaction with available services and economic pressure to provide more and better services resulted in a restructuring of the bureaucracy that governed telecommunications policy. New firms entering the telecommunications market in China in the 1990s created the same competitive pressures.

Early New Entrants: The Great Wall, Jitong, and Unicom

The first to organize serious competition against the telecom ministry's monopoly was the People's Liberation Army (PLA). In the beginning of economic reforms in the early 1980s, before the military was banned from commercial ventures, the PLA operated businesses to help generate income to cover budget shortfalls. As do most militaries in the world, the PLA controls certain electromagnetic spectrum allocations and rights to the radio waves, a necessary resource for wireless communications. In the mid-1980s, the PLA entered the wireless telecommunications market, particularly paging—a lucrative business at the time.[6] The PLA was not subject to oversight from other government departments and was exempt from MPT and other government regulation. These commercial operations were often local ventures run by regional military units.[7] In the mid-1990s, the PLA and China Telecom entered into a joint venture, known as Great Wall, to provide commercial wireless telephony service in Beijing and Shanghai.[8]

However, military leaders found that the corruption and declining professional standards engendered by commercial enterprises were more corrosive than the financial benefit to military units.[9] In July 1998, President Jiang Zemin ordered the military to cease all commercial operations. Regional military units had three years to make the transition; local military districts were ordered to sever ties as soon as possible. At the time, there were 20,000 military enterprises in China, which tended to enjoy preferential regulation and were not subject to control by other government departments.[10] The government ordered Great Wall to hand over its wireless operations to Unicom.

In 1993, the State Council approved the establishment of Unicom, a second carrier organized to compete with China Telecom in cellular, local, and long distance service, and a third carrier, Jitong. This was partly in response to consumer demand and partly to satisfy the ambition of ministries interested in sharing in the profits telecommunications service could generate.[11] MEI was the primary backer of both Jitong and Unicom. As recounted by Mueller and Tan, since the 1960s a combination of policies—the self-reliance ethos that encouraged each ministry to provide for itself, the tendency of ministries to build their own empires, and the inability of the MPT to meet demands for telecommunications service—resulted in a proliferation of private networks to serve the internal needs of their owners. The PLA and the Ministries of Railways, Electric Power, Transportation, and Petroleum had exceptionally extensive telecommunications networks for their own use. Several of these ministries sought to commercialize their private telecommunications networks. The private networks were supplied by equipment produced by MEI. Before the opening of the market to foreign equipment, MEI's companies were more technologically advanced than the manufacturing ventures of MPT. However, MPT's public network became more important than the private networks as economic growth spurred development in the 1990s. Demand for public telecommunications services grew, MPT's pricing policies created the capital necessary for significant increases in investment, and MPT entered into joint ventures with foreign manufacturers to supply the equipment to feed this growth. As MPT became more important as a manufacturer of equipment, its importance relative to MEI also increased. In part to rebalance this relationship, MEI ventured out of the equipment market and also sought opportunities to enter into the services market.[12]

In 1993, the State Council allowed the creation of Jitong to administer the Golden Bridge Projects, which included the building of China's early Internet network. More than twenty government agencies participated in the State Joint Conference, which was supported by a working office directed by an MEI vice minister.[13] Jitong began service in January 1994. Its primary customers were large state-owned enterprises. Jitong established a satellite network that interconnected with MPT's network, serving such users as the Ministries of Water, Transportation, Forestry, Marine, and Petroleum.[14] Jitong's entry into this value-added data services market was relatively easy, as it was not a direct competitor to China Telecom and it received important political backing as a symbol of the Chinese elite's conviction that science would modernize China.[15]

Unicom was a different story. Although the State Council had given Unicom approval in 1993 to enter telecommunications, not until 1995 did Unicom begin providing any services, and then only cellular service in a small number of cities. Fundamentally, its problem was a regulatory one. One of China Telecom's tactics was not to provide enough telephone access numbers to Unicom.[16] Another was to refuse to interconnect with Unicom's network, meaning that Unicom's customers would not be able to communicate with anyone on the China Telecom network. Unicom's general manager, Li Huifen, accused MPT of failing to grant Unicom interconnection to China Telecom's mobile phone networks. "The compatibility of the Global System Mobile [GSM] phone networks in four cities was solved only when leaders of the State Council intervened personally," she said of Unicom's service in Beijing, Tianjin, Shanghai, and Guangzhou. In 1998, five years after Unicom received its license and three years after beginning service, Lu Jianguo, vice president of China Unicom, said, "The biggest problem facing our further development is the connection with local networks owned by China Telecom."[17] The government thus began considering more drastic approaches to resolve the complaints.

China Considers Structural Separation of the Old Monopolist

As other countries liberalized their telecommunications markets, China Telecom continued to face a steady stream of consumer complaints. There were enough complaints about excessively high connection fees for new subscribers to inspire lawsuits across the country. Users complained to not only domestic but also international media about expensive prices and poor service. Even then Premier Zhu Rongji was reportedly unhappy with the state of competition in telecommunications.[18] It was in this atmosphere that rumors swirled about the possible restructuring of China Telecom and Unicom. In December 1998, the influential news magazine *Caijing* reported this familiar complaint:

> In Beijing, the installation fee was higher than 6000–7000 yuan [US$723 –$843]. At that time people told a joke: "the Americans don't eat and drink for ten months to buy a car; the Chinese don't eat and drink to install a telephone." Until the first half of 1997, in Beijing the average waiting time for a telephone was greater than 36 days. China Telecom's workers seemed to leave an unhappy impression on every customer, including a high ranking MII official—a former secretary of the minister—visited by this reporter. Although there were ever-emerging indicators of China Telecom's very large waste, there was never any reliable evidence, because although it is a public corporation, China Telecom nevertheless never released its financial information. Among Chinese "dinosaur" industries, originally known as the "Iron Big Brother," the Ministry of Railways shrank because of competition with the highways and airlines, leaving China Telecom as the lead dinosaur.[19]

The magazine went on to identify consumers' five major complaints about telecommunications service: installation fees were high; rates for international calls were high; waiting lists for telephone installation were too long; customer service was poor; and everywhere the tallest building was always the telecommunications building, a physical monument to the company's enormous profits.[20] In this environment of dissatisfaction and complaint, the government began considering how to restructure the market.

In principle, there are two approaches to structural separations: vertical separation and horizontal separation. Vertical separation seeks to separate the incumbent's activity in a competitive market from its activity in a non-competitive market. For example, in telecommunications, the market with the highest cost of entry is the local telecommunications service, especially the provision of a telephone to each individual consumer, the part of the network known as the "local loop." In a typical home, the local loop is that part of the network from the consumer's telephone handset to the first major gathering point for all such lines from that neighborhood. Most other parts of the telecommunications market, such as long distance, national backbone service, and wireless service, have lower costs of entry and in many countries are thriving competitive markets. Therefore, vertical separation in telecommunications suggests that an incumbent's local network would be separated from the parts of the network that would provide service long distance and wireless markets, which are competitive.

The advantage of vertical separation is that it prevents an incumbent from using revenues from the monopoly market—in this case the local loop market—to subsidize service in competitive markets—in this case long distance and wireless markets. If the incumbent is able to cross-subsidize its participation in competitive markets, it has the ability to set prices below the cost of providing the service and can potentially drive out all other competitors in that market. Regulators can intervene to prevent such cross-subsidization by dictating prices, but obtaining correct cost information from a single incumbent that has every incentive to dissemble is very difficult.[21] Typically, only when there is a powerful regulator and a very strong respect for the rule of law can a regime accomplish such a task.

An alternative to vertical separation is horizontal separation, which divides an incumbent into smaller sections, each of which may still participate in competitive and noncompetitive segments of the market. A common type of horizontal separation is the restructuring by geographic region. In a pure horizontal separation in telecommunications, for example, an incumbent could be separated into an eastern company and a western company. Each new company could provide local, long distance, and wireless services. The government could choose to allow east and west to compete in each other's geographic territories. The advantage of horizontal separation is that it preserves economies of scope between the competitive and noncompetitive segments of the market. Furthermore, from a regulator's point of view, where there was previously only once source of information on costs and other data necessary for regulation, now there are automatically two sources. This can increase the level of transparency for data, which is essential for regulatory decisions.

Various forms of structural separation have occurred in the world of telecommunications. In the United States, when AT&T was divested, it was broken both into long distance and local services—a vertical separation—and the local services component was further divided along geographic lines—a horizontal separation. Known as the regional Bell operating companies, these new units were confined to local service within their geographic region and were not permitted to enter competitive segments of the market—namely, long distance and wireless. Not until new legislation passed in 1996 were regulations loosened to allow them to become more vertically integrated companies. In Japan, the incumbent NTT has always remained a vertically integrated carrier; however, the government has required accounting separation between different units. Initially, these units were separated vertically—with demarcation lines between wireline, NTT, and wireless operations, known as NTT Docomo in 1992. In 1999, the government required further division within the company—both a vertical separation by dividing long distance from local, and a horizontal separation, by dividing east from west. However, in the case of Japan, all these divided units remain under a single holding company, unlike in the United States. Canada has both separation of long distance from local and separation by region. Argentina split its incumbent into northern and southern companies. Brazil also has several regional telecommunications companies. Thus, by the late 1990s, China had a handful of examples it could look to in making its decisions about China Telecom.

During the debate about the separation of China Telecom, in the summer of 1998 the newly created MII submitted two proposals to the State Council on how to create competition by dividing China Telecom either vertically along business lines—data, wireless, satellite, and paging—or horizontally along geographic lines. Unicom was also asked to send in industry reform proposals.[22] Liu Cai, then head of MII's law and planning office, reportedly preferred that China Telecom be divided according to business lines rather than along geographic lines. The division along business lines was consistent with the analysis provided to MII by financial advisors that separation of China Telecom along business lines would result in the highest possible value should the company list on foreign stock exchanges. Others, concerned about China Telecom's international ranking, argued that separation by business lines would preserve in one unit China Telecom's fixed line operation and maintain its relatively high rank as one of the largest telecommunications companies in the world.[23]

Still others, including Beijing University professor Zhou Qiren, who had been visiting the United States at the time AT&T's acquisition of Comcast, which joined one of the largest American telecommunications and cable companies together, strongly believed that the best way to introduce competition in telecommunications was to allow the Internet and cable television networks to compete against China Telecom.[24] This argument, premised on technologies that enable disparately developed networks to provide like services, implicitly challenges not only the economic organization of the Chinese telecommunications industry but also the political organization of the industry, by suggesting that aspects of the propaganda apparatus—namely, the cable television sector—are not special ideological services but are instead commercial commodity services, like telephone service. Similar ideas were considered in MII.

MII Minister Wu, in February 1999, suggested that there would be three kinds of networks—audio, video, and data—that could be provided by fiber. He further noted that the networks of telecommunications, broadcasters, railways, and electricity all had fiber in some portion. He proposed that the networks could be owned by different organizations but that oversight responsibility for all of them would be assigned to MII. In the area of cable television networks, for example, SARFT would retain responsibility for managing the content that flowed over the network, but MII intended to regulate the network itself.[25]

From November 1998 through January 1999, there was a series of meetings and conferences, some of which included the ministries, companies, and academics with expertise in the area, to discuss how the market ought to be restructured. While these meetings were in progress, the liberalization of Hong Kong's international telecommunications service market took place on January 1, 1999. The incumbent international services carrier, Hong Kong Telecom, was immediately forced to defend its dwindling market share by cutting prices. Hong Kong Telecom began offering a 30 percent discount on all calls to northern China, which comprised about 60 percent of Hong Kong's outgoing international calls. Its average revenue per minute fell by 25 percent. A competitor to Hong Kong Telecom, New World Telecom, cut its late-night prices for international service by 60 percent.[26] With these highly publicized market developments occurring in Hong Kong, the general conclusion of these conferences in mainland China was that it could not escape the effect of market competition; reform was necessary to preserve the competitive strength of China Telecom relative to other telecommunications companies; and necessary to domestic reform of the telecommunications industry was a timetable for opening the industry to international competition.[27] In April 1999, MII Minister Wu announced that China Telecom would be divided into four companies along business lines—a fixed, a mobile, a paging, and a satellite company (see Figure 4.1).[28]

Around the same time, reports emerged that Premier Zhu had decided that China Telecom would first be divided along business lines, but as a part of a larger plan. After two years, these smaller companies would be divided again along regional lines, thus ending any one company's monopoly—this change eventually occurred in 2002.[29]

After the 1999 structural separation, China Mobile grew rapidly—more rapidly, many believe, than if it had remained tied to China Telecom.[30] The separation of China Mobile from China Telecom reduced the latter's incentive to stonewall Unicom's wireless operations. Now, China Telecom was obliged to offer similar terms to both China Mobile and China Unicom. As of 2003, although China Mobile had more subscribers than did Unicom, because of the nature of the split with China Telecom, China Mobile actually had less of a national backbone than Unicom, meaning that China Mobile relied more on China Telecom for interconnection services than did Unicom. Many believe that splitting

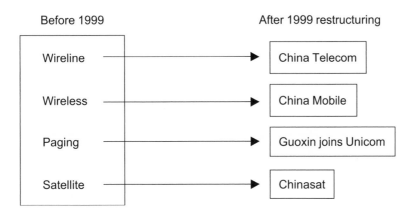

FIGURE 4.1 China Telecom restructuring, 1999

China Mobile from China Telecom evened the competition between the two mobile operators, setting the stage for price wars and incredible growth in mobile subscribers.

Railcom Enters, Tentatively

The Ministry of Railways has the second most extensive communications network after China Telecom, has its own national backbone network, and provides both local and long distance services to its railway offices. Other carriers, such as Jitong and Unicom, were customers of the Ministry of Railways network.[31] In 1999, when China Telecom was restructured and the government's focus was on strengthening its competitors, allowing the railway communications system to enter the commercial market was an attractive proposal. Initially, it was proposed that the ministry's extensive national wireline network partner with Unicom's national wireless network to form a company that could compete with China Telecom in all market segments.[32]

However, there were serious challenges to the merger of the railway network and Unicom. First, although the Railways Ministry's network was extensive, it had only 1 percent of China Telecom's capacity.[33] Additionally, in order to merge with Unicom, the communications network would need to be separated from the operation of the railways. The Ministry of Railways would have to transfer 60,000 to 70,000 workers. However, they were not organized into a single administrative unit but instead were still constituted within the regional offices of the railways operation.[34] The entirety of the Unicom work force was not more than 10,000 workers, not including the 20,000 workers from the Guoxin Paging Company, which had been assigned to Unicom as part of the China Telecom restructuring. Unicom wanted the Ministry of Railways network but not its employees.[35] Perceiving that a poorly managed merger of the railways network and Unicom could result in Unicom's collapse, MII offered an alternate proposal: that the railways enter the telecommunications service market on its own. If productivity improved after three years, a merger with Unicom could be reconsidered.[36]

In December 2000, China Railway Telecom was awarded a license to offer to the public services that included fixed lines, long distance, Internet, and data communications. The company has access to rights of way along the railway tracks, valuable property rights that operators such as Unicom lack.[37] By May 2001, Railcom began trial operations in Beijing and Shanghai. Commercial operations began in June 2001 with about two million subscribers, mostly railway staff, who were located near railway stations.[38]

Although Railcom had enough support to get licensed, other forces—perhaps at MII—were working against it. MII documents on Railcom's entry suggested that its telephone service charges could be 20 percent lower than China Telecom. On March 16, 2001, Railcom placed ads in Beijing's *Morning Paper* to promote its service packages but was immediately challenged over its listed prices. The following report was published in the influential newsweekly *Caijing*:

> This reporter has received confirmation from MII that it is investigating the rates Railcom printed in the paper. Although according to MII's principles of asymmetry for non-dominant carriers and new carriers, Railcom should have the privilege of offering rates at a 10 to 20 percent discount, just because that is how the document with the "red stamp" reads, there is no guarantee that what ought to happen will actually happen. Railcom is waiting, and its competitors are waiting. According to a knowledgeable source, the case of Railcom's newspaper ad is not just about the price, but also includes the way Railcom used to open up a market for itself, for example offering to large users a fixed general use fee.[39]

As was common practice in 2001, Railcom planned to charge installation fees of 680 yuan (US$82). Although this fee was less than China Telecom's installation rate, it would help Railcom cover the cost of expanding the network. However, in early July 2001, MII cancelled installation fees nationwide. Although cancellation of the installation fee was a popular move, MII also eliminated one of the competitive advantages Railcom would have had in the market at a key moment in its development.[40] On the interconnection front, not surprisingly given the experience of Unicom, Railcom has faced difficulties. Over a year later, in August 2002, Xinhua news agency reported: "China Unicom and China Railcom, the two underdogs in China's telecommunications market, had filed innumerable complaints on the poor quality of interconnection between their networks and that of China Mobile and China Telecom." These complaints include accusations that rivals were cutting communication cables and changing settings on switchboards.[41]

Netcom Enters, Aggressively

In October 1998, Hou Ziqiang of the Chinese Academy of Sciences began building support for the development of an experimental fiber network to provide broadband Internet service. He found backing from Shanghai Telecom, the city office of China Telecom; Shanghai Investment Company; and the Ministry of Rails. In November 1998, this group reported its proposal to the State Council. It needed capital to invest in the project and permission to construct the network, which would replicate the coverage of other networks, if not the services offered by others. The idea reached Premier Zhu Rongji's office at the time when discussions related to China Telecom's restructuring were at their height. Premier Zhu, at a meeting of the State Council in February 1999, decided that the project should be not an experiment but a commercial venture. Although Hou Ziqiang, the initiator of the project, was doubtful about its commercial prospects, the project went forward as Netcom, a new telecommunications operator.[42]

China Netcom (CNC) was formally established in October 1999. Four investors each had 25 percent stake in the company, with registered capital of 120 million yuan (US$14.46 million). The Railways Ministry and the SARFT offered their networks as part of their capital investment, although Netcom had the freedom to use or not use these networks as it saw fit.[43] The Chinese Academy of Sciences, with the backing of the State Planning Commission, was responsible for the management of the network. Netcom focused specifically on providing wholesale carrier-to-carrier services, not on providing commercial services to individuals. Its core offering would be IP services over its IP backbone.[44] Within two months of getting its license in August 1999 and with the backing of foreign manufacturers, Netcom had built its national IP backbone, to the surprise of China Telecom.

Once Netcom's IP backbone was in service, Internet service providers in China had two options—to lease from China Telecom or from Netcom. This competitive pressure freed Unicom to also accelerate its backbone development.[45] On November 15, 1999, Netcom began a trial offering of IP telephone service in fourteen cities in China, a shift toward retail as well as wholesale services. On March 30, 2000, Netcom received a license to offer IP telephony. In May 18, 2000, Netcom was licensed to offer international services.[46]

Netcom attracted key individuals. Edward Tian, a political outsider, was selected to be chief executive officer of Netcom because of the success of his Internet services venture AsiaInfo,[47] an American company founded by students from China who were educated in the United States. In 1995, AsiaInfo won a contract to build out Chinanet, the largest commercial Internet network in China. By 1997, AsiaInfo controlled more than 70 percent of China's Internet node servers, with points in all thirty-one provinces and autonomous regional capitals and self-governing cities.[48] Also involved in Netcom was Jiang Mianheng, who had studied electrical engineering in the United States and is the son of former President Jiang Zemin. As supervisor of the Shanghai city government's office of information technology, one of Netcom's investors, Jiang Mianheng was involved in several high technology projects in Shanghai.[49]

Netcom also attracted foreign investors. Through special petitions to the State Council, Netcom received permission to bring in foreign capital through a private offering. Private investors, including Newscorp's Rupert Murdoch and Goldman Sachs, poured US$300 million into Netcom's operations. Foreign investors held 15 percent of Netcom's stock as of October 2000, nearly a year before China's WTO foreign participation commitments in the telecommunications would become clear.[50]

At the end of 2000, Netcom gave the impression of having all the advantages: the best technology, the most market-oriented management, and the highest political support.[51] However, by November 2001, there were reports that Netcom's strategy as a "carrier's carrier" had failed. Competing with China Telecom on network leasing had been too difficult, despite its good political connections.[52]

China Telecom Splits Again in 2002, and Netcom Reemerges

Despite the vertical separation of China Telecom in 1999, it was China Telecom's old units—China Telecom and China Mobile—who were performing the best. Every other carrier—Unicom, Netcom, Jitong, Railcom—was struggling. Starting in early October 2001, there were rumors in the media of a proposal to split China Telecom into northern and southern companies.[53] At stake were several issues: whether the other carriers would be reconfigured;[54] whether carriers without mobile licenses would get the licenses, and whether the licenses would be issued immediately or later;[55] and whether MII would be replaced. One rumor was MII would be replaced by a regulator and that the State Council Informatization Office, which would be combined with MII and SARFT, would serve as a transitional organization to such a regulator.[56] Whether firms would be allowed to freely enter and exit the market did not appear to be under consideration at all.

However, in late December 2001, China Mobile and China Unicom share values dropped in Hong Kong on fears that China Telecom would gain a mobile license.[57] One senior official described the several options considered in the second restructuring of China Telecom. The original plan was to divide China Telecom into a long distance company and five local companies. This kind of separation would further isolate the least competitive market—local service—from the long distance market, which could be competitive and was now likely to be subsidized from revenue generated in China Telecom's local service. The second option was to split China Telecom into three large companies, trying to bring together those provinces most alike in economic development and teledensity levels. In practice, this would have resulted in some kind of east, west, and central separation. The most developed company, remaining vertically integrated in fixed line services, could prepare first for a listing on stock exchanges. The others could follow suit when ready.[58]

The final option was the decision was to split China Telecom into a northern and southern company.[59] The southern company would retain the China Telecom name and about 70 percent of the network. The northern company would be merged with Netcom and Jitong and would retain 30 percent of China Telecom's fixed network. One State Council official stated that the north-south line had been drawn to achieve a balance of human and capital resources. Compared with the southern part of the company, the northern part of China Telecom was less responsive to consumer demand—integrating north China Telecom with the more market-oriented Netcom and Jitong would be beneficial, State Council officials believed.[60]

One of the largest state-owned enterprises in the country, China Telecom has 500,000 employees,[61] 250,000 of them in the northern region. Netcom, by contrast, has 3,000 employees.[62] Neither China Telecom nor Netcom received a mobile license, despite MII Minister Wu's earlier promises, suggesting that in the end this kind of decision was beyond the authority of the minister.[63] The split and merger process began in early 2002 and took a year and 100 billion yuan (US$12 billion) to complete.[64] As of March 2003, although most of China Telecom had been split, negotiations over the division of some of the network were still underway.[65]

The challenges facing Netcom in the merger of north China Telecom, Netcom, and Jitong are significant to the point that one Netcom executive could not definitively say whether the company would contribute to or burden the government treasury. Although on the surface the three entities merged, in practice each had licenses to provide certain services to the exclusion of others—and these distinctions remain. Table 4.1 summarizes these differences. Big Netcom refers to the former northern

Table 4.1 Overlap of Netcom (Big and Small) and Jitong, 2002

	Big Netcom	*Small Netcom*	*Jitong*
Fixed local	Permitted	Only in 5 provinces and one city	
Long distance	Permitted	Only in 5 provinces and one city	Permitted
International	Permitted	Only in 5 provinces and one city	Permitted
Data	Permitted	Only in 5 provinces and one city	Permitted
IP network		Only in 5 provinces and one city	Permitted
Internet service		Only in 5 provinces and one city	Permitted
Leased line		Only in 5 provinces and one city	
Broadband Internet service		Only in 5 provinces and one city	

section of China Telecom, encompassing eleven provinces. Small Netcom refers to the original Netcom, which is now permitted to operate in five provinces, Anhui, Hubei, Hunan, Jiangxi, and Fujian, and one city, Shanghai. Small Netcom retains the foreign investment of the original Netcom. Jitong has a national license that is, however, limited to a few services. As a result, in some cities, a year after the merger, all three subcompanies of Netcom were competing against each other to provide certain services—such as long distance.[66]

From several interviews of Chinese officials and analysts, it appeared that MII was marginalized in the decision-making process for the second restructuring of China Telecom. At least one source stated that flatly that because MII had participated in the licensing of Unicom and the subsequent first structural separation of China Telecom, both of which had failed to achieve robust competition, when the decision was being made on the second structural separation of China Telecom, MII was not consulted. The State Council and State Planning Commission were the key organizations in the finalization of the second structural separation plan for China Telecom.[67] The State Council's objective appears to have been the transformation of China Telecom into smaller competitive operators while maintaining some stability for the hundreds of thousands of current workers in the industry.[68] In parallel, with WTO commitments in place, another government objective is to allow domestic companies to enter the market as competitors on an equal or earlier time frame than foreign companies. One official believed that the second restructuring of China Telecom would not be the final one. He predicted that another restructuring of China Telecom and of the bureaucracy that oversees telecommunications would occur in the next few years.[69]

Indeed, by 2005, serious rumors were circulating about the future of Unicom and wireless licensing in general. Both China Telecom and China Netcom wanted to participate in the wireless market. In contravention of regulations, they introduced Little Smart (*Xiaolingtong*) service, which offered consumer wireless terminals to fixed telecom network service, a phenomenon discussed in Chapter 8. Only the possibility that a license for the more technologically advanced third generation (3G) mobile service would be awarded dampened China Telecom and China Netcom's interest in moving forward with Little Smart. 3G technology is designed to offer data service, as compared with the second generation (2G) technology, used by Unicom and China Mobile, which primarily offers voice service. At this time, the Chinese government expressed a commitment to developing a home-grown 3G technology, known as TD-SCMA. Therefore, coupled with the issue of assigning 3G licenses was the question of which operator would be permitted to use which 3G technology and which operator might be required to use TD-SCMA, commercially less proven than the two standards most widely used internationally: CDMA 2000 and W-CDMA. Unicom has two mobile networks, one CDMA network upgradable to CDMA-2000 and one GSM network upgradable to W-CDMA. The rumor was that Unicom would be split—its CDMA network given to one of the wireline operators along with a 3G license and its GSM network given to another wireline operator along with the second 3G license. China Mobile would receive a third 3G license in this plan. China's telecom market would then be dominated by three large operators, each with a mobile business, rather than by four operators. In May 2008, after years of rumors, the government announced its third plan for restructuring the industry. Three operators would remain, China Telecom would take over Railcom and Unicom's CDMA mobile network. Unicom, with its GSM mobile business, would merge with China Netcom. China Mobile would remain the third operator. As an incentive, the government would award each of these three companies a 3G license upon completion of the restructuring.[70] There is no discussion of operators making such decisions on their own based on their commercial interests; there is no question that they do not have such influence over their own futures—only the state retains that privilege.

Within the space of ten years, a variety of firms entered and exited China's telecommunications market, but none did so without the express backing of a ministry and the State Council. The following list of carriers who entered also notes their supporters:

- Great Wall, backed by the People's Liberation Army
- Unicom, backed by the MEI (1993)
- Jitong, also backed by the MEI (1993)
- China Mobile, which was split from China Telecom, the incumbent (1999)

- Chinasat, which was also split from China Telecom (1999)
- Railcom, backed by the Ministry of Rails (2000)
- Netcom, backed by the Chinese Academy of Sciences, the Shanghai municipal government, and two ministries (1999)

The following are those carriers who exited:

- Great Wall's wireless operations were merged with Unicom (1998)
- Jitong was merged with "new Netcom" (2002)
- Netcom was merged with the northern portion of China Telecom into the "new Netcom" (2002)

Worldwide there are a variety of approaches to letting new firms in to the telecommunications market (see Figure 4.2). Open markets like the United States take approach one. Liberal markets such as Hong Kong, Japan, and Australia, take approach two. More closed markets such as Taiwan take approach three. China, however, takes approach four. Only firms that have the support of the State Council and its ministries may enter the market. Therefore, as much freedom as these firms may have in the market, the market itself is not open because of the highly restricted entry conditions. This is consistent with other studies of the Chinese

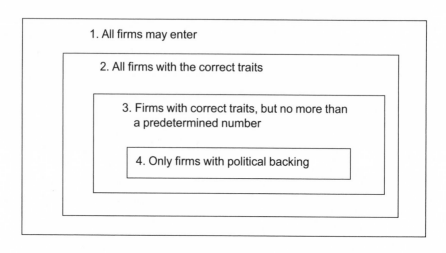

FIGURE 4.2 Different approaches to new entry

state as a system of bureaucratic actors that reach decisions by striking bargains with each other.[71] Although licensing is an area where the state expresses total control, in each successive case the state's ability to influence developments decreases, suggesting that for major decisions to be reached, bargains must be struck. However, as subsequent cases will demonstrate, the more technical detail a decision requires, the less able any unit, including the ministry, is able to govern effectively. The following chapters focus on other policy areas—foreign investment, interconnection, retail pricing, and technological innovation.

5 Foreign Investors
Caught Between State and Company Demands

In essence, the recent story of foreign investment in China's telecommunications market is largely one of great foreign interest pitted against substantial Chinese resistance. As one foreign businessman in the Chinese telecommunications market once said to me, in China there are two great uncertainties about the regulatory regime: one never knows, first, when the rules might change and, second, when the existing rules will be enforced.[1] In the 1990s, international telecommunications firms had substantial capital to invest outside their home markets. During this time, although the Chinese government officially banned foreign investment in telecommunications, it often relaxed and enforced these rules unpredictably. The successful initial public offering (IPO) of China Telecom shares on the Hong Kong and New York stock exchanges in 1997 opened new opportunities for foreigners to invest in state-owned firms, but in a manner that minimized their management control. The conclusion of China's accession agreement for WTO membership at the end of 1999 began the codification of a new set of foreign investment rules. Following the collapse of the global telecommunications market in the second half of 2000, few foreign companies had new capital to invest. With China's telecommunications service market now officially open, the country must compete with other markets for a smaller pool of funds.

China's approach toward foreign investment in telecommunications service is to maximize the influx of advanced technology and—for some companies—capital, while minimizing the influence of foreign companies. When foreigners petitioned to introduce the telegraph in China in the nineteenth century, Chinese officials resisted all efforts to establish such networks in their country. However, as discussed in Chapter 2, some officials, including the prominent reformer Li Hongzhang, saw this ban as a futile exercise. Li believed that as the technology evolved, either foreigners or even the Chinese would illegally establish networks. Given that the telegraph was faster than the imperial courier, Li believed that eventually the government itself would have to establish a network. Later, the Qing dynasty did begin to build its own telegraph network as part of its defense against Japan's growing military power.[2] Foreign companies also continued to build telecommunications and telegraph lines, until an exasperated imperial official, Yuan Shikai—later briefly the president of the Republic of China—proposed that the emperor take over all telephone and telegraph facilities outside the foreigner- controlled treaty ports. Toward the end of the Qing dynasty and through the subsequent Nationalist period before World War II, the government nationalized all telecommunication services in China and placed them under the management of the MPT.[3]

There was no further foreign investment in telecommunications services in China until reforms in the 1980s began altering the fundamental structure of the economy. Whereas in other industry sectors—even in telecommunications equipment manufacturing—foreign investment grew, it remained prohibited in telecommunications services. The typical rationale given for the ban was well articulated in November 1999 by Geng Zhicheng, of the MII's Research Institute of Telecommunications Intelligence:

> It is certain that the entry of foreign funds will have a negative impact on China's information security. The United States can enter Iraq and collect information there under the cloak of the United Nations; how it is possible they can behave themselves when they are in the center of China's nerve system. The entry of foreign funds into China's telecommunications market is a grim challenge to China's information security.

Perceiving the inevitable effect of WTO membership, Geng further suggests,

Under the premise of not affecting the investment enthusiasm of foreign businessmen, we should strictly restrict the degree of participation of foreign investors in the telecommunications enterprises. The main reasons for this are: first, state security and stability are the fundamental conditions for social economic development. As the state's nerve center network, the telecommunications industry is the key to maintaining the political stability of the country.[4]

Foreign companies at this time were eager telecommunications investors everywhere in the world, including China. Interestingly, foreign observers and Geng agree on one point—greater transparency and certainty for foreign investment were necessary. Foreigners want transparency and certainty to protect their investment. Geng wants transparency and certainty in order to attract the foreign management skills and technology necessary to improve telecommunications services.

China is not alone in its reluctance to allow foreign participation in the telecommunications service market. As recently as the mid-1990s, many countries, especially developing countries, were reluctant to allow foreign investment in telecommunications for a variety of sovereignty-related concerns. Scholar Steven Globerman noted that major categories of concern included a desire to retain telecommunications profits for a domestic operator, worry about compromising national security, and hope that a domestic owner would promote social objectives that may not be directly profitable.[5] Although Globerman concludes that there is no evidence that limiting foreign ownership of telecommunications is necessary to achieving any of these goals, political resistance to foreign investment still exists.

Other studies suggest that the size of the market is an indicator of a country's approach to foreign investment, although it is not clear whether large size favors more openness or not. In a comparison of Australia, New Zealand, France, Germany, and the United Kingdom, by Australian scholar Richard Joseph, the larger markets proved more open to foreign direct investment because these countries had operators that sought to enter other countries' markets. Although all the larger countries—Germany, France, and the United Kingdom—exhibited historical concerns about losing national assets and compromising national security, these concerns were counterbalanced by an interest in reciprocity—should they open their markets to foreign companies, there would be an expectation that other countries might do the same for their companies.[6]

However, a broader study by Georgette Wang suggests that income levels in addition to market size are indicators of what approach a country will take toward foreign investment in telecommunications. Low and low-middle income nations, of whatever size, tend to be more open to foreign participation because they have little domestic industry to protect and an urgent need for investment and technology. High income countries may have domestic industries to protect but are also more likely to have domestic operators that are internationally competitive and would seek opportunities to invest abroad. Middle income countries that have large domestic markets and a domestic industry that is not competitive in global markets are the most likely to have strict foreign ownership controls.[7] China is just such a country.

Changing Winds of China's Foreign Investment Regulations

Before China joined the WTO, foreign investment in telecommunications services was banned. However, there were a number of state-approved arrangements that would give foreign investors an opportunity to participate in the market. One early example was the Tianbo company, established in Hong Kong by the MPT in order to attract foreign investment capital to develop China's telecommunications network. According to China Telecom, "Foreign investors may set up a joint investment firm with MPT's overseas companies, such as Hong Kong-based Tianbo, to initiate investment in mainland's post and telecommunication projects which will be operated by the mainland's post and telecommunications authorities when completed. The foreign investor will harvest returns according to bilateral agreement."[8] In 1993, however, Liu Guangqian, director of Tianbo and former director of the MPT policy and legislation department, felt obliged to reiterate that the ban on foreign investment in China's telecommunications industry had not changed. Liu further stated:

> The main reasons China imposes restrictions on opening of its telecommunications industry to the outside world are as follows. First, China's domestic telecommunications level is still at a low level and development in different areas is dreadfully imbalanced; therefore, the telecommunications industry in China is not aimed at gaining profits, but

at providing services for a comprehensive development. Second, because the telecommunications industry's characterized by "a whole course [*quancheng*] a comprehensive network and a concerted operation," all localities are required to develop in a technically well- coordinated way and adopt an overall auditing system.[9]

Basically, foreigners were not allowed in because the government wanted to maintain total control over technical planning of the national network and to be able to transfer funds from profitable services to subsidize unprofitable ones.

A later example of the shifting winds on foreign investment is found in the Internet market. In their early years, major Chinese websites, such as sohu.com and sina.com, reportedly relied almost entirely on foreign investors for capital. Foreign companies such as Yahoo!, Intel, and Goldman Sachs have invested an estimated US$100 million in Internet service providers and Internet content providers, despite the lack of clarity surrounding the legality of such investments. However, in September 1999, soon after the announcement of Yahoo!'s investment, MPT Minister Wu surprised industry representatives by insisting that foreign investment in Internet content providers was illegal and that the ministry would enforce these rules as necessary. Minister Wu also announced that a licensing system would be imposed on Internet content providers and that the government would monitor the content of websites.[10] Through late December 1999, weeks after China's WTO accession agreement had been reached and it was widely known that foreign investment would be permitted in telecommunications services, MII Minister Wu continued to threaten a crackdown on such projects. However, in early January 2000, Wu reversed positions, stating that foreigners were permitted to own up to 49 percent of the shares in telecommunications service providers, including Internet service providers, in a limited number of cities, upon China's accession to the WTO. The percentage would rise to 50 percent two years later, and the number of cities would expand over time.[11] This storm over foreign investment in the Internet in 1999 and 2000 is only a microcosm of the numerous conflicts that have erupted over foreign investment in telecommunications over time.

By far the most egregious example of shifting rules in telecommunications foreign investment was the case of Unicom and the Chinese-Chinese-Foreign (CCF) arrangements (see Figure 5.1). The Ministry of Power and the Ministry of Railways established Unicom in 1994, but because of coordination problems between the ministries, Unicom could not use the ministries' networks' excess capacity and instead chose to build its own network. Consequently, Unicom required rapid and large infusions of cash. Unicom used the CCF mechanism to bring foreign capital into the company. A Chinese company that could have a foreign joint-venture partner then also arranged to be a partner of Unicom. Essentially, a Chinese company was used as an intermediary between Unicom and the foreign company to circumvent the rules prohibiting foreign investment in telecommunications services.[12] Unicom needed funds in the face of competition from well-financed China Telecom and used a CCF arrangement to expand its limited access to capital.

Unicom's behavior suggested that the government's policy toward foreign investment had relaxed. MPT official Wang Jianrong drew a fine distinction: "Foreign investors can help build networks and recoup their investment with a portion of the profits . . . But they can't hold an equity stake and receive dividends, though, because that would mean they have a part in operations."[13] Minister Wu Jichuan in 1995 echoed this posture, saying that foreign companies could invest in telecommunications projects but only "under the precondition that they will not hold equities or be involved in the operation or management of telecommunications business . . . First, there's the question of sovereignty, and, secondly [*sic*] the fact that information touches on commercial secrets."[14] Around forty-six companies, including Deustche Telekom, France Telecom, and Sprint, invested around US$1.4 billion in Unicom through CCF arrangements.

FIGURE 5.1 The Chinese-Chinese-foreign (CCF) arrangement

They were permitted to derive revenue from installation fees charged for building new lines, not from services.[15]

Starting in mid-1997, however, Minister Wu Jichuan began rejecting more forcefully the possibility of foreign investment in telecommunication services. "We still have difficulties in letting foreign counterparts get involved in China's telecommunications service sector because the conditions are not ripe . . . Foreigners, when they come, are after profit. As minister, I would not like to share policy-based profits with them." Wu mentioned such projects as an optical cable from Lanzhou to Llasa, linking two of the poorer areas of China, and postal services as examples of projects cross-subsidized by other telecommunications services.[16]

Toward the end of 1998, as the government's lukewarm acceptance of CCF arrangements for Unicom chilled, it appears, primarily as a result of two developments: a highly successful IPO by China Telecom in 1997 and the acceleration of China's WTO accession talks toward their conclusion. In October 1997, the cellular operations of China Telecom in Guangdong and Zhejiang province were established as "China Telecom (Hong Kong)," and its shares were listed in New York and Hong Kong stock exchanges. As *Newsweek* reported:

> The lines formed before dawn. Struggling office clerks, retirees, civil servants, and high-powered investors crowded outside Hong Kong banks last week to snap up applications to buy shares in the city's hottest new stock issue . . . Everybody hoped for huge returns from the biggest public offering yet of a mainland-controlled company. Government worker Simon Soo posted family members at banks around town to grab as many applications as possible. "China is a great market," said Soo. "I forecast profit."[17]

China Telecom (Hong Kong) sold 25 percent of its shares in the listing, raising US$4.22 billion. The other 75 percent remained owned by the Chinese state. At the end of 1997, it was the fourth largest company listed on the Hong Kong exchange.[18] In June 2000, this became part of China Mobile, as part of the split of China Telecom in 1999.[19] The success of this company in attracting foreign capital created hopes that other Chinese telecommunications carriers could do the same—raise foreign funds without ceding control to foreign investors.

In 1998, the media reported that an internal government document was circulating in which was proposed a ban on Unicom's CCF arrangements. Despite the telecommunications ministry's earlier justifications for CCF, the ministry now began to assert that CCF was essentially a structure to circumvent the ban on foreign investment.[20] MPT First Vice Minister Liu Jianfeng, a major Unicom supporter, left MPT. Finally, given China's weak economic growth at the time, domestic Chinese banks were willing to lend to telecommunications industries, one of the few sectors that continued to grow.[21]

As China's WTO accession talks progressed in the summer of 1998, the lack of alignment between China's principled stance against foreign investment in telecommunication services, for national security and sovereignty reasons, and the actual practice of several kinds of foreign joint ventures, began to compromise China's negotiating position. The State Council reportedly noted two particular projects as the most egregious circumventions of the foreign participation rules: Unicom's US$60 million project in two Guangdong cities with France Telecom and Unicom's US$72.3 million wireline project in Tianjin with Sprint.[22]

Finally, toward the end of 1998, Minister Wu announced, "China Unicom has started to use the Chinese, Chinese, Foreign method. But in this method we have found many irregularities . . . these are violations of development laws. At the moment, we are conducting a process of rectification . . . We want to clean up these joint ventures one by one." In direct contradiction to previous statements, Minister Wu said that foreign companies in CCF ventures should not be deriving their revenue from installation fees, as installation fees were implemented in order to subsidize network build-out in less developed areas.[23] While MII was engaged in cleaning up the Unicom situation, then Premier Zhu Rongji at a March 1999 news conference during the Ninth National People's Congress affirmed China's overall telecommunications strategy: "China Telecom is reducing prices, but I don't think that the reduction is far enough. I think prices should be reduced continuously. The way to do this is to introduce competition. First, we are reforming the system of China's telecommunications industry by breaking the monopoly and encouraging competition. Second, is to open up China's telecommunications market to foreign investors in a step-by-step manner."[24]

Starting in July 1999, Unicom began issuing to its foreign partners letters detailing the termination of the CCF ventures, paving the
way for a Unicom IPO in 2000.[25] On August 30, 1999, MII officially
announced that CCF arrangements were illegal and ordered that Unicom resolve them. Unicom had in effect forty-six agreements developed
over fifteen years, which included cooperative arrangements with over
thirty large telecommunications companies from over ten countries. By
the end of September, Unicom had not resolved its CCF arrangements,
but because of an MII decree, revenues ceased to flow to foreign investors on October 1.[26] Foreign investors were incensed; several governments lodged protests with the Chinese government. These conflicts
occurred in parallel with the close of negotiations on China's WTO accession arrangements.

China's WTO Telecommunications Commitments

On November 15, 1999, China concluded its WTO accession
agreements. China's commitments with regard to foreign participation
in telecommunications services are shown in Table 5.1.[27]

When on November 15, 1999, China's WTO accession agreement
was reached, which included plans for legal foreign investment in telecommunications services, MII and Unicom's negotiating position weakened and agreements accelerated.[28] By December 1999, Unicom had
reached agreements with most of its foreign partners on terminating the
CCF ventures, including companies from Japan, Korea, the United States,
Canada, and Europe. By February 5, 2000, Unicom had "in principle"
agreements with Bell Canada, the American International Group, and
CCT Telecom Holdings. Analyst reports at the time indicated that large
companies with other interests in China to protect settled first but that
most held out for better terms, threatening legal action and possibly jeop-
ardizing Unicom's intended foreign listing. Among them was Singapore
Technologies, a Singapore government-owned company that had invested
with Unicom over 300 million yuan (about US$36 million) in paging
ventures in twenty-one Chinese cities. As part of the WTO accession
agreement talks, the European Commission extracted a concession that
allowed France Telecom, Siemens-Deutsche Telekom, and Telecom Italia
to reinvest later in Unicom the capital these companies were being re-

Table 5.1 Commitments on foreign investment in telecommunications

Type of service	Upon WTO succession (12/2001)	1 year later (2002)	2 years later (2003)	3 years later (2004)	4 years later (2005)	5 years later (2006)
Value-added	30% in Beijing, Shanghai, Guangzhou	49% in 17 cities	50% with no geographic limits	———————————————→		
Basic telecom-mobile	25% in Beijing, Shanghai, Guangzhou	35% in 17 cities	————→	49% with no geo-graphic limits	————→	
Basic telecom services-fixed	0%	0%	0%	25% in Beijing, Shanghai, Guangzhou	35% in 17 cities	49% with no geographic limits

quired to remove.[29] In retrospect, Edward Snyder, Chase H&Q's senior telecommunications analyst in San Francisco, described the CCF saga:

> Back in 1994 when fledgling Unicom was struggling for funds to compete with behemoth China Telecom, it devised a scheme to skirt a ban on foreign investment in telecom operation . . . But early last year [1999], and three Unicom chairmen down the line, the deals were stopped by a government ruling. Unicom offered to return initial invest-ments at an average rate of 6 percent—returns on telecom deals are usually nearer 30 percent. It also told its foreign partners to accept or face being shut out of the market in the future. The result? Unicom acquired foreign management skills and the use of capital at very little cost to itself.[30]

After the resolution of the CCF arrangements, Unicom became the second Chinese carrier to list on foreign exchanges. In June 2000, China Unicom Limited went public and raised US$5.65 billion in the New York and Hong Kong Stock exchanges, the biggest IPO in Asia at that time outside of Japan. Only the most promising sections of the com-pany were brought together as China Unicom Limited for the foreign offering: its cellular businesses in Beijing, Shanghai, Tianjin, Guang-dong, Jiangsu, Zhejiang, Fujian, Liaoning, Shangdong, Anhui, Hebei, and Hubei; and its long distance, data, Internet, and Guoxin paging services. Left out were its cellular operations in other regions; its wireline local networks in Tianjin, Chengdu, and Chongqing; satellite; and Unicom paging businesses.[31] In short, approximately 22 percent of China Unicom Limited's shares were sold to the public; the remainder is owned by the Unicom Group—which is entirely owned by the Chinese state.

Around the same time, in mid-2000, *South China Morning Post* reporter Willy Wop-Lam reported that then President Jiang Zemin, Premier Zhu Rongji, and State Councillor Wu Yi were dissatisfied with the preparations of the ministries for WTO accession. Zhu's instructions were that state firms merge to form companies that would be competitive against multinationals two to three years after WTO accession. However, President Jiang reportedly was concerned about some sectors: "in areas such as telecommunications, we must do our best to protect not only our economic sovereignty and well-being but also national security." After China's entry into the WTO, Jiang had been advised that it would become more difficult to control politically subversive material that could flow over telecom, the Internet, and media. As a result, Lam reports one source as saying that "the leadership is anxious to have regulatory and quasi-censorship mechanisms put in place before [there is] sizeable foreign participation in the telecom, media and related fields."[32]

With the drama surrounding Unicom's CCF arrangements just subsiding, in 2001 Netcom had a private placement for foreign investors. In order to get permission for this foreign investment that year, after the China's WTO accession agreement was reached but before the foreign investment rules went into effect, Netcom sought approvals from the State Council, the Ministry of Economic Reform, and the Ministry of Foreign Trade and Economic Cooperation (MOFTEC). Thirteen percent of the company was offered. Of the total foreign investment in Netcom, 80 percent came from two sources: Rupert Murdoch's News Corporation and Goldman Sachs. By the second quarter of 2003, nearly a year after Netcom's merger with the northern part of China Telecom, the status of this foreign investment, including the influence of the investors, was still under discussion.[33]

China's Regulations on Foreign-Invested Enterprises were approved by the State Council on December 5, 2001, and went into effect on January 1, 2002. Telecom enterprises with foreign investment must have registered capital of 2 billion yuan (US$240 million) to invest in basic interprovincial service, 10 million yuan (US$1.2 million) for value-added interprovincial services (this includes Internet services), 200 million yuan (US$24 million) for basic intraprovincial service, and 1 million yuan (US$120,000) for value-added intraprovincial service. The major Chinese participant in the venture must demonstrate that it has sufficient capital and management to undertake the services promised and must comply with industry requirements set out by the regulator. The major foreign participant must have a telecommunications license in its country of incorporation and have a good performance record in the provision of basic telecommunications services. This appears to exclude foreign investors that are not telecommunications companies. The venture must submit a project proposal, a feasibility study, and other relevant credentials and certificates. The application must be examined by the local telecommunications authority, and the application is then forwarded to the State Council. It must also be examined by the local foreign trade and economic cooperation department and then forwarded to the State Council foreign trade and economic cooperation department.[34]

As of March 2003, two years after China acceded to the WTO, there was only one telecommunications service project with significant management control by the foreign investor—AT&T's Symphony. The project's history begins, however, well before China became part of the WTO. AT&T was a long-time partner of China Telecom in providing international telecommunications services between the United States and China. In the 1990s, AT&T focused its potential investment interest in Shanghai, where it had business customers. When Zhu Rongji became premier, the project idea was welcomed more warmly, and in 1994, AT&T signed a framework agreement with the Shanghai city government to move forward. Progress was interrupted by the 1995 split of then AT&T into three separate companies—AT&T services, Bell Labs (now Telecordia), and the telecommunications manufacturing section (now Lucent).

In 1997, AT&T pursued the project further and submitted to the State Council a proposal to invest in the construction of a high-speed network in Shanghai. Instead, Shanghai Telecom built it themselves. The following year, AT&T modified its proposal to provide only broadband services to multinational corporate customers in the Pudong district of Shanghai, a special economic development zone. This project would involve no investment in basic infrastructure but rather only an overlay network to give customers a higher performance service.

On March 31, 1999, just before then Premier Zhu Rongji traveled to the United States to discuss China's WTO accession agreement, the Shanghai Posts and Telecommunications Administrative Bureau signed an agreement with AT&T for the latter to provide telecommunications services in Pudong. The agreement was submitted to the State Council for approval. MII Minister Wu called the project a "breakthrough" in the opening of the telecommunications service market to foreigners.[35] On December 4, 2000, AT&T and the Shanghai Information Investment's joint venture, Shanghai Symphony Telecom, was established. The venture was to offer broadband Internet service to international companies with offices in Pudong. In keeping with China's commitments, a Chinese partner was to retain controlling interest. In the case of Shanghai Symphony, the partner chosen was Shanghai Telecom, part of China Telecom, and the main competitor of the joint venture. Not surprisingly, although AT&T and the second Chinese partner, Shanghai Information Investment, actively supported beginning operations, Shanghai Telecom was noncommittal.[36] For the two years following the project's approval in 2000, regulatory challenges and Shanghai Telecom's opposition prevented services from commencing. MII wanted to require the venture to rely on a Chinese Internet service provider to connect to the global Internet instead of leasing an international private line, which AT&T believed would be more reliable. It was essentially a ruling that would degrade the possible quality of the joint venture's service. Eventually, a compromise was reached, and services were launched successfully in March 2002.

China Telecom's 2002 IPO: Seeking Capital Without Strings

After Unicom's big IPO success in 2000, a newly restructured China Telecom—just separated from its mobile unit—began looking for opportunities to list on the market again. The challenge was deciding what portion of China Telecom would be attractive to foreign investors. Originally, the plan was to list all the provincial operations south of the Yangtze (Changjiang) River—Jiangsu, Zhejiang, Guangdong, and Shanghai—plus Beijing and Shandong in the north. However, by June 2001, it was clear that further telecommunications reforms were under way, and there was the possibility that China Telecom would be broken up via a horizontal structural separation. This meant that Shandong and Beijing could not be included in the market offering, which substantially reduced the number of operations that would be attractive to list. The IPO plans were delayed until matters cleared. In 2002, the newly split China Telecom retained operations in twenty-one provinces, but the eleven provincial operations in China's southwest and northwest regions were unprofitable. After the split was complete in August 2002, China Telecom submitted applications to U.S. and Hong Kong authorities to list on the stock exchanges.[37]

China Telecom's IPO was delayed more than once in 2002.[38] Although telecommunications service in China continued to grow, foreign interest in the market was negatively affected by the poor conditions in the international capital market, especially for telecommunications ventures. As Figures 5.2 and 5.3 show, starting in mid-2000, the value of Chinese telecommunications stocks dropped sharply.

Yet, China Telecom insisted on an IPO in October 2002 in the midst of a global recession. When asked about the purpose of China Telecom's IPO, one China Telecom manager intimately familiar with the IPO process explained that it was not to raise capital but rather to increase its ability to make its own management decisions. Said another manager of a competing firm, if a company has shares listed on foreign stock exchanges, then the company can explain certain decisions—for example, the need to reduce the number of employees—as necessary to meet the demands of the capital market. Otherwise, the company is at the mercy of the government's decisions.[39] This is consistent with Barry Naughton's view of the cyclical nature of economic reforms in China— that allowing a free market price to compete with a state-controlled price encourages new entry into markets, more price flexibility, and incremental managerial reforms.[40]

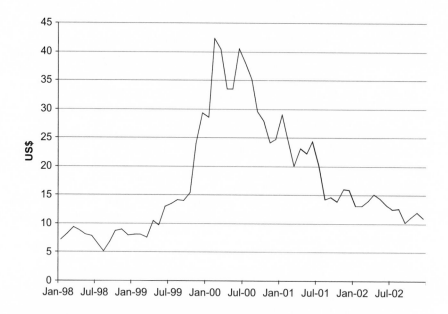

FIGURE 5.2 China Mobile's stock value, 1998–2002
SOURCE: finance.yahoo.com

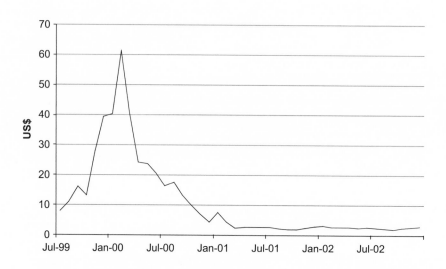

FIGURE 5.3 China Unicom's stock value, 1999–2002
SOURCE: finance.yahoo.com

China Telecom's first IPO effort in the October 2002 collapsed. The financial media reported the failure to attract sufficient buyers, despite the incentives offered by the government, as a blow to China's general program of seeking foreign capital to restructure state-owned enterprises. In early November, the MII tried to enforce the accounting rate, which is the wholesale rate foreign carriers pay China Telecom to terminate international calls in China. The accounting rate had existed at a very high level for years but had been widely, illegally circumvented, which had resulted in quite competitive and low consumer retail rates for international calls to and from China. MII's sudden effort to actually enforce the accounting rate threw China's international service market into disequilibrium: "The decision has caused uproar in Hong Kong where many people believe it was politically motivated and aimed purely at increasing investors' interest in the China Telecom share issue. Some analysts said Premier Zhu Rongji was determined to push for the flotation despite a weak market because he wanted to complete the reorganization of the mainland's telecommunications sector before he left office in March 2003," said the *South China Morning Post*.[41] After halving the size of its offer to 7.56 billion shares, China Telecom successfully launched its IPO in mid-November of 2002.[42] The global telecommunications fever of the late 1990s that had made China Mobile's and Unicom's IPOs so successful had vanished, and China Telecom in 2002 was forced to compete fiercely against other projects for foreign capital.

Despite the uncertainties, foreign firms are continually trying to gain a foothold in the mainland market. In 2005, Netcom and Hong Kong telecom incumbent Pacific Century Cyberworks (PCCW) were invested in each other: Netcom bought a position in PCCW, and PCCW bought 50% of Netcom's broadband business in two provinces.[43] That same year, Spain's incumbent Telefonica also took a position in Netcom.[44] Also, the United Kingdom's Vodafone bought 3 percent of China Mobile.[45] Then, in December 2006, the State Council's SASAC released a statement that several strategic industries, telecommunications among them, would remain dominated by state-owned enterprises. The statement was a warning to foreigners not to expect relaxation of foreign participation rules in the designated sectors, despite the temptations that may be offered by officials willing to bend the rules.[46]

In the area of foreign investment, there are few ways for firms to maneuver within the limited scope of activity granted by the government or to escape the authority of the government on any meaningful scale. The government has largely succeeded in making the necessary foreign investment liberalization commitments to gain WTO membership while creating conditions that practically discourage any significant participation in the telecommunications services market. Therefore, in the foreseeable future, it is unlikely that any major foreign investment in the telecommunications services market will occur, leaving all the best market opportunities to the major state-owned operators. As one Chinese Telecom official stated in spring 2003, three years before he had been worried about the entry of foreign investors. Now he felt no need to be afraid—as the global telecommunications market weakened, China Telecom strengthened, taking most of the market for itself. Only the niche markets were left for the foreigners.

Conclusion

Chinese firms seek technology and capital from foreign investors—thus explaining China Telecom's early efforts with Tianbo, Unicom's adventure with CCF arrangements, and Netcom's private placement. Foreign investment is also a tool for Chinese state-owned enterprises to dilute the state's management influence, as revealed by China Telecom's pursuit of public offering despite a poor economic climate. However, the government resists ceding profits or management control to foreigners—thus the rationale for ending Unicom's CCF arrangements and the push toward listing companies on foreign stock exchanges to bring in foreign capital without foreign management influence. AT&T's Symphony project demonstrated how China resists foreign investment in infrastructure if it comes with foreign management control, in contrast to other developing countries that need foreign investment as a primary means to build basic infrastructure. Finally, WTO talks accelerated the demise of CCF arrangements. Often the liberalization and future openness promised in the rhetoric leading up to the WTO commitments were in direct contradiction to the government's actions taking place concurrently in the telecommunications market. Figure 5.4 illustrates these gaps between the government's commitment and actions. Although the gap between the permissive, explicit rules and the actual barriers in foreign investment rules may be intentional, they reflect a more general credibility problem in China's regulatory regime. If firms do not understand when rules will change or whether existing rules will be enforced, there is little incentive to follow any rules at all. China's telecommunications regulatory regime lacks certainty, as demonstrated by these foreign investment rules and in Chapters 6, 7, and 8 on interconnection, pricing, and new technologies.

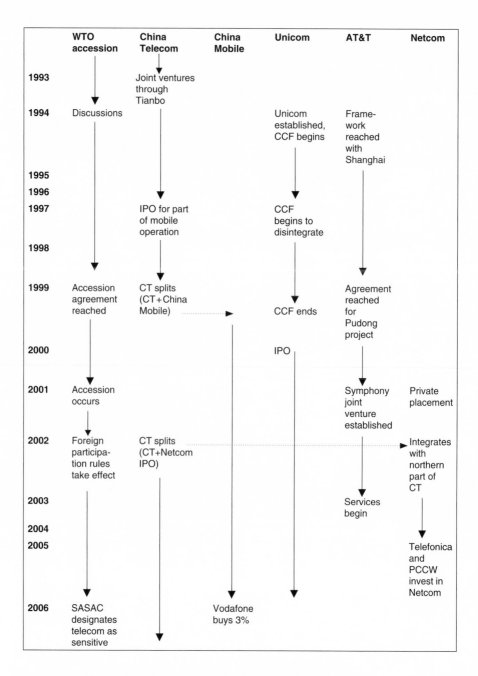

FIGURE 5.4 History of foreign investment in telecommunications services

6 The Heart of Competition Policy in Telecommunications
Making Interconnection Work

Making interconnection work among operators is key to the modern competitive telecommunications market. At the beginning of the twentieth century, when telephones were still in their infancy, competing operators did not interconnect. A small business might need to subscribe to service from several telephone operators because on each line one could call only subscribers on that network, not subscribers to other networks. When the technology was new and not considered a social and commercial necessity, the lack of interconnection was not a problem. However, today consumers expect to be able to call from one telephone anyone else who has a telephone, even if the party they are calling is on a different operator's network. This is possible only because operators, even those that compete with one another, interconnect their networks.

The story of interconnection in China, as is the case in many countries, involves a string of disputes and their resolutions, an ever evolving series of government-issued rules and procedures, and a mix of government institutions with varying capacity to handle the disputes in line with the rules that have been issued. The state has not yet succeeded in establishing a regulatory framework for interconnection that operators are willing to use, which creates market uncertainty that favors the most powerful operators. MII possibly lacks commitment both to competition and to the fair treatment of all carriers. It definitely lacks the cost data from the firms to make good interconnection pricing decisions. It may further lack the technical skill to process the data in order to strengthen the interconnection regime. In short, the interconnection regime in China is weak, and that vacuum is filled by the most powerful operators moderated only by occasional State Council fiats.

In a monopoly environment, no interconnection regime is required. However, in a multioperator environment, interconnection is important, and because an incumbent operator is unlikely to interconnect voluntarily, explicit rules that govern interconnection are necessary. Interconnection rules typically detail several major categories of conditions.[1] For example, there is often a set of legal obligations that identify what kind of operator is required to provide interconnection, the procedures an operator must follow to request interconnection, and a dispute resolution mechanism to manage conflicts among operators. Also, there are often technical rules that identify the minimum points in the network where interconnection should take place; furthermore, operators with market power are often obligated to lease additional essential elements of their network to other operators, and time frames are often indicated for delivering these technical services. Finally, there are usually rules that establish a standard for setting prices for interconnection. These can be specific prices, price ceilings, or prices based on economic cost models.

This chapter traces the course of several interconnection disputes in historical order, marked by discussion of the existing rules. In China, the government introduced competitors into the telecommunications market in 1993, prior to establishing any interconnection rules. In 1995, MPT issued some initial technical specifications for interconnection. In 1999, MII issued provisional interconnection rules, which are still in effect today. The Telecommunications Decree of 2000 contains some language on interconnection, largely focusing on dispute resolution procedures. In the meantime, the government's successive decisions to divide China Telecom, once in 1999 and a second time in 2002, can be interpreted as the use of structural separation as a tool to prevent anti-competitive conduct in recognition of the failure of the rules-based interconnection regime. Finally, this chapter concludes with a discussion of the role and relevance of the several government actors involved in interconnection problems—the State Council, the telecommunications ministry, and the provincial communications administrations.

Interconnection in China: Resolution by Divestiture

In China, interconnection is a relatively new policy area in telecommunications. Prior to the entry of Unicom into the market, there was no need for an interconnection regime. The need for an interconnection regime began in 1993, when the State Council agreed that several ministries could establish a joint venture to introduce a second operator, Unicom, into the telecommunications market. Owned by MPT, China Telecom made every effort to block the development of China Unicom by resisting network interconnection, a common behavior among telecommunications incumbents in many countries. At this time, MPT tried establishing regulations and provisions for interconnection. However, these rules were never enacted due to the lack of established laws and friction between MPT and MEI.[2] At this time, China Telecom was still a department within MPT, and its financial and personnel issues were fully controlled by this ministry. MPT was responsible for the financial performance of China Telecom.[3] As a result, the quality of service Unicom was able to offer suffered, and the company experienced great difficulties in maintaining its mobile telephony subscribers.[4]

In June 1995, MPT issued some technical specifications for interconnection, but problems persisted. Two years after it was initially established, Unicom was finally able to begin providing mobile services in late 1995. However, interconnection negotiations with China Telecom for both fixed and mobile services foundered on the pricing of interconnection charges. China Unicom mobilized political interest to bring the dispute to the State Council. In 1994, in order to coordinate better interconnection issues, the State Council established the State Joint Conference on National Economic Information, which was later replaced by the National Information Infrastructure Steering Committee in 1996. Chaired by a vice premier, with participation from MPT and the various ministries involved in China Unicom, it was unable to resolve these conflicts effectively. Eventually, the State Council authorized the State Planning Commission instead of MPT to arbitrate the dispute. A compromise on interconnection was issued in March 1996.[5]

This problem was echoed in Unicom's only wireline venture at the time, a network in the city of Tianjin. In July 1997, Unicom completed its investment in a local phone network in Tianjin, a 600 million yuan (US$72.3 million) project, undertaken in a fifteen-year partnership with the American company Sprint and the Japanese firm Sumitomo.[6] However, a year later, the Tianjin company had still not received interconnection with the local China Telecom network and, therefore, had not been able to begin operations.[7] In May 1998, China Unicom was successful in getting aired on China Central Television (CCTV) an hour-long documentary that showed how China Telecom's Tianjin operation, with the support of MPT, had significantly delayed the deployment of Unicom's service in that city. The program included interviews with Unicom's Tianjin customers complaining about delays. The general manager of Unicom and former vice mayor of Tianjin Li Huifen was said to have used her influence to get the program aired.[8] Unicom opened its local telephone network in Tianjin on July 19, 1998.[9] Unicom charged an installation fee of 805 yuan (US$97), a substantial discount compared with China Telecom's standard fee of 3700 yuan (US$446).[10] By September 1998, Unicom had 3,000 fixed telephony subscribers in the city.[11] A few months later, by early 1999, Unicom's subscribership had increased to 500,000.[12]

In March 1998, a reshuffling of government responsibilities and the separation of China Telecom from MPT improved the interconnection climate. MPT was merged with MEI, Unicom's major patron ministry, and a State Council office, to form the new MII.[13] As a result, Unicom's subscriber numbers increased rapidly.[14] Finally, on October 29, 1999, MII announced the first set of rules related to interconnection, "Provisional Regulations on the Administration of Telecommunication Network Interconnection."[15]

The provisional interconnection regulations, which apply to wireline and wireless communications networks, identify the relevant organizations that participate in interconnection discussions, outline procedures for filing interconnection agreements with MII for approval, and detail dispute resolution measures if a commercial arrangement cannot be reached. The rules establish that interconnection between operators should begin within seven months of an initial request for interconnection or within four months of a request for expansion or modification of arrangements. All interconnection agreements must receive approval from MII, and such agreements must be filed with the local communications administrations. The provisional regulations list nine areas of possible dispute, including interpretation of the rules, technical requirements, time frames for provision of services, quality of service, and financial settlement issues. If there is a dispute, either MII or the local administration can initiate coordination among the parties. The MII or local administration must begin coordination within fifteen days of receiving the request. There are several stages to the coordination:

- First, the coordinator can consider the views of both parties, undertake inspections, and propose a solution. If the solution is not accepted, the case moves to the second stage of coordination, which involves seeking outside expert opinion and proposing another solution.
- If this fails as well, then views from operators' headquarters at a national level are solicited, and another solution is proposed. The entire proceeding must be completed in thirty days.
- If still no agreement is reached, then the MII or local administration has another sixty days to simply issue an administrative decision.[16]

In principle, therefore, disputes should be resolved in 105 days from the time they are referred to the government.

The new rules improved Unicom's ability to provide service. The interconnection agreements Unicom reached with China Telecom after the establishment of MII expanded Unicom's scope of service, quickened the procedures necessary to get interconnection, lowered interconnection rates, and improved technical specifications. Unicom previously was limited to offering mobile services, IP telephony services, and local service in the cities of Tianjin, Chongqing, and Chengdu. However, with changes in its interconnection agreement, Unicom was permitted to build and operate its own international network and no longer was required to rely on China Telecom for these services. Unicom began providing both domestic and international long distance in March 2000. However, there were still certain limitations on these services. Unicom offered long distance service only from twenty-five large and medium-sized cities. Consumers could not subscribe to the service directly and needed to dial a code, 193, ahead of the area code.[17]

Improved interconnection streamlined the procedures Unicom was required to follow to provide service in individual local areas. Unicom's per-three-minute-unit cost of interconnection and its construction costs for establishing physical interconnection points were reduced. Technical specifications that constrained Unicom's construction decisions and efficient use of deployed equipment were relaxed. For example, previously in each local calling area Unicom was required to build a mobile switching center, to route telephone calls from the calling to the receiving party. After the interconnection framework improved, a single mobile switching center could be used for more than one local calling area, reducing Unicom's equipment and construction costs. As a result of these changes in the interconnection framework, the quality of service Unicom was able to provide its subscribers substantially improved. Between 1998 and 1999, China Unicom's subscribership tripled from 1.4 million to 5.2 million.[18]

Telecommunications Decree of 2000: Incremental Improvement

To strengthen the provisional interconnection regime, language in the 2000 Telecommunications Decree further detailed the processes for implementing interconnection. The decree firmly states that an incumbent cannot refuse an interconnection requirement of any service operators or leased-line operators, thus strengthening the obligation of operators with market power to offer and abide by interconnection agreements. The decree also set out more detailed procedural rules:

- Interconnection agreements should first be undertaken as a commercial negotiation between the parties.
- If these parties are unable to reach an agreement within sixty days of the initial request, a party can then apply to an administration for arbitration.
- The administration has fifteen days to begin action on the request for arbitration.
- If through arbitration parties still do not agree within forty-five days, the administration can issue a decision, after consultation with experts.[19]

- In the event that the proposals resulting from coordination among the parties and consultation among experts are not accepted, then the responsible office must issue an administration decision within sixty days.
- Finally, if there are violations of the rules, local administrations can issue warnings and penalties of 5,000–30,000 yuan (US$625–US$3750).[20]

These rules vary somewhat from the provisional rules. Nevertheless, even with the decree, disputes ought to be resolved within 120 days of a complaint being brought before a government administration.

After the 2000 Telecommunications Decree was issued, China Unicom applied for interconnection for long distance, international, and IP telephony, expanding its scope of service further. Not happy with the offer it received from China Telecom, it resubmitted its application to MII in February 2001. MII notified Unicom that it would have its interconnection rights by March 2001. The government resolved this dispute within one month and publicized it as an example of how it would operate.[21] In October 2001, China Telecom and China Unicom signed another interconnection agreement. China Telecom spokesperson Si Furoung said, "It is also one of our preparations for the pending harsh competition after the country opens the telecommunications market to overseas companies."[22]

In 2002, a newly constituted Netcom, combining part of the incumbent network with a new competitive entrant network, also experienced interconnection struggles. In a discussion with Netcom executives, who were part of the old Netcom prior to the restructuring of the company, even as late as 2003 Netcom was still primarily in the position of asking for interconnection from China Telecom. China Telecom disrupted Netcom's business by periodically breaking interconnection— three hours one day, three hours another day, and at other unpredictable times. As the disruption was apparently random, China Telecom was not easily held accountable for such behavior. Meanwhile, the disruption was enough to hurt Netcom's ability to maintain a high quality of service to its customers.[23]

In negotiating interconnection agreements, one of Netcom's strategies was to offer China Telecom certain terms and conditions in northern China, where Netcom owns the wireline network, on condition that

Netcom receives the same conditions in southern China, where China Telecom controls the wireline network. One of the direct benefits of splitting the old China Telecom into a northern and southern network is the possibility to compare behavior and prices of the two networks against each other. However, in the particular case of interconnection, Netcom in its initial years did not have much success with this strategy.[24]

Under the improved regime, in January 2002, China Railcom reached interconnection agreements with all other operators. Railcom had already begun business a year earlier, and without the interconnection agreements, it had struggled. A Shanghai official confirmed in mid-2002 that Railcom more than any other carrier was having a particularly difficult time with interconnection agreements, which severely curtailed its business prospects.[25] Railcom's difficult experience, even with the improved procedures under the 2000 Telecommunications Decree, demonstrated that difficulties in China's interconnection regime remained.[26]

In 2002, an interconnection dispute flared between China Mobile and Unicom over interconnection with Unicom's newly built code division multiplex access (CDMA) networks, the technology that it had inherited the right to deploy from Great Wall, the joint venture of China Telecom and the People's Liberation Army. China Mobile's irritation over interconnection terms with Unicom has some historical roots. When Unicom was established in the mid-1990s, China Telecom's mobile operations had reached a "bill-and-keep" interconnection arrangement with Unicom. By international standards, bill-and-keep is a fairly typical interconnection arrangement and means that there is no payment settlement between two carriers for interconnection; rather, each operator recovers all its necessary costs from its own customers. However, the background that led to this arrangement in China between mobile operators is unusual. Unicom needed interconnection with China Telecom's mobile operations, but China Telecom was unwilling to build the facilities necessary to make that interconnection possible. Unicom offered to make the substantial investment needed to build the necessary facilities on the condition that it would not have to pay traffic usage charges for interconnection. China Telecom accepted this offer, believing that Unicom's, and mobile operators' traffic in general, would not rise to high levels. Thus, the bill-and-keep settlement arrangement was established between the mobile operators. No interconnection charge on a per-minute basis was charged by either carrier to the other carrier.[27]

As the mobile market grew, so did Unicom. The old interconnection agreement that had once favored China Telecom's mobile operator, now known as China Mobile, now favored Unicom. The significant increase in the volume of traffic Unicom generates, which terminates with China Mobile, has likely increased pressure on China Mobile's network capacity. However, given the agreement established early on, China Mobile has not succeeded in changing its fundamental interconnection arrangement with Unicom.[28]

In preparation for China Unicom's launch of its new CDMA network, a cellular network that would use a kind of transmission technique that was different from the networks already then deployed in China, the two operators reached a new interconnection agreement for their mobile networks in 2001. MII officials attended the signing ceremony for the agreement in November of that year. The media reported that "China Unicom and China Mobile vowed in the agreement to carry out in-depth cooperation with modes competition," despite the fact that fierce rivalry at the local level had led to constant complaints that the other operator was violating tariff rules and despite the general reluctance of China Mobile's provincial subsidiaries to link their networks with China Unicom's.[29]

This ongoing friction between the two mobile operators was one of the deep-seated problems revealed in interconnection disputes in Henan Province. In 2002, Unicom invested 280 million yuan (US$33.7 million) in a CDMA network in Nanyang, a city of 500,000 people, one ninth of the population of Henan Province. That year Unicom signed up 42,000 subscribers, but as of January 2003, it was down to 25,000 subscribers. However, Unicom found that even among those remaining subscribers, only about 8,000 actually used the network. By February 2003, it was attracting not even ten new subscribers a day, said a local Unicom executive.[30]

The cause of Unicom's trouble was lack of interconnection with other networks. One customer said that she had subscribed to Unicom CDMA, but because her phone calls were not getting through, she had returned to China Mobile. In October 2002, Unicom conducted a survey of 1,240 subscribers. Only one person believed it was possible to use the CDMA service to get a call through to a Nanyang Mobile (part of China Mobile) subscriber more than 60 percent of the time. Ninety percent of those surveyed said they could not get through more than 30 percent of the time. Throughout Henan Province there was an enormous volume of complaints. In most of the cities in Henan, Unicom experienced a connection rate of less than 30 percent—in other words, in ten attempts to make a phone call, seven attempts failed to connect.[31]

In 2002, Unicom lost 5,400,000 RMB (US$650,000) on this network. With its survival at stake, on May 21, 2002, Nanyang Unicom brought before the Nanyang Intermediate Court a case against Nanyang Mobile that alleged unfair competition, a novel recourse for interconnection cases in China. However, the government intervened, and the case was brought before the Henan provincial telecommunications administration office; a year later, it was still unresolved. China Unicom appealed to the State Council, in hope of resolution of the problem. On May 23, 2002, under the leadership of then Premier Zhu and Vice Premier Wu Bangguo, MII Vice Minister Zhang Chunjiang chaired a meeting of operators on interconnection. By meeting's end, there was stated a clear demand that operators complete interconnection with Unicom's CDMA network by October 1, 2002. However, within a week, Unicom again appealed to the State Council, reporting that interconnection continued to be blocked and asking for a higher level decision. Between September 27 and 30, 2002, Vice Premier Wu Bangguo and Premier Zhu Rongji responded to that appeal, demanding that MII investigate the case and solve it. This resulted in MII Minister Wu Jichuan's call for an MII work meeting in early 2003, the end result being a demand that all carriers work toward better interconnection and the directing of MII's efforts toward improving the interconnection regime.[32]

Which Government Institution Has the Authority?

Interconnection disputes place a heavy burden on provincial communications administrations. On paper, the dispute between China Mobile and Unicom should have been resolved by the local communications administration. When Unicom appealed to the Nanyang Intermediate Court for review, the case was sent to the Henan Communications Administration. Evidently, the Henan administration, like some other provincial administrations, was unable to effectively manage the inter-connection rules. In the end, these conflicts were often presented to the State Council for resolution.

For telecommunications officials in China, interconnection work is relatively new. The most fundamental problem appears to be marshalling the people with specialized, technical skills to implement the interconnection rules that exist. The major telecommunications companies in China employ tens of thousands of people. By contrast, the local communications administrations are very small. Provincial telecommunications administration offices sometimes have as few as ten employees. Offices this size are doing well if they can afford to devote two employees to interconnection disputes.[33]

In 2002, when I visited officials from three local communications administration—Shaanxi Province, Guangdong Province, and Shanghai—they all identified interconnection disputes as one of the major issues that they face. Although MII in Beijing was separated from China Telecom in 1999, local telecommunications administrations were separated from China Telecom's provincial operations only in 2001, which complicated the relationship between the regulator and the regulated companies. Most of the regulatory staff typically were former personnel of China Telecom. The Shaanxi Telecommunications Administration, which I visited in Xian in April 2002, had thirty people altogether. The Shanghai Communications Administration, which I visited in June 2002, also had about thirty employees but devoted seven to dealing with interconnection.

Although it was relatively newly established, of the three local administrations I visited, the Shanghai Administration was the surest in its procedural framework. As one officer described it, there are three aspects to handling interconnection disputes: the law, the rules, and public relations. Also, there are three teams of people who handle interconnection issues in Shanghai. First, there is the decision-making leadership, a committee of high-ranking executives from each of the companies. Second, there is a working group where each company sends a representative who has authority for everyday management of the company. This group meets every four months to handle routine problems. Third, there is a scholars' group, which meets to discuss the latest interconnection problems, provide education, talk about experiences, and help companies try to better meet the demands of other companies. The activities of these groups are funded through fees levied on the companies.[34]

According to the Shanghai officials, at every meeting of the working group there is a required monthly report, which includes data on dropped connections, traffic statistics, and other traffic reports. The administration analyzes the numbers and publicizes them at the meeting. If errors are too high, the group tries to reach some understanding of problems at this quarterly meeting. For example, representatives to the working group may try to ascertain whether the problems are caused by equipment or other resources. If the problem persists for three months, the Shanghai Communications Administration reports this to Beijing. Of course, the Shanghai officials said, they try to resolve problems in Shanghai, but if the problem is not resolved in a timely way, they are forced to report to Beijing. Reporting to Beijing also means informing the Beijing headquarters of the telecommunications operators. For the local Shanghai offices of these companies, a report to company headquarters in Beijing is an embarrassment and something to avoid; therefore, the threat of a report is relatively effective, according to the Shanghai Communications Administration. As a result, the administration had not needed to report any big interconnection problems, except for the new and relatively small operator Railcom, which was having trouble working with China Telecom.[35]

In contrast, other local administrations said that their interconnection problems were quite severe. In the western province of Shaanxi, the Communications Administration officers reported that interconnection agreements were well established but that companies refused to honor them. Operators bring disputes to them, they said, but they have difficulty determining whose views are correct. The questions they raised reflected basic misgivings about the empirical data given to them by the operators. In Guangdong, the communications administration officials were particularly concerned about how to set appropriate interconnection rates, an area in which the provisional rules and the Telecommunications Decree are vague.[36]

All the provincial communications administrations said that their enforcement powers were weak. Although they could issue fines, the fines are so small they are not effective deterrents against bad behavior by operators. As the Shanghai administration pointed out, all the operators are government owned; therefore, forcing operators to pay fines paradoxically means that the government is fining itself. In Shaanxi Province, a personal element intervened. As recently as 2001, China Telecom's workers were part of the provincial telecommunications administration. Although now separated, the remaining government officers found it personally unpleasant to constantly issue fines to their former colleagues.[37] At the national level, said one MII official, MII and the provincial telecommunications administration offices have issued hundreds of fines, but to little effect.

MII states that it is going to deal with the interconnection problem, although its ability to enforce the related rules and guidelines is limited. Between 2001 and 2003, there were over ten formal interconnection disputes, mostly at the provincial level. Two disputes brought by operator headquarters have been referred to MII, say government officials.[38] Somewhat cynically, and revealing the ministry's deep-seated frustration, one MII official observed in an interview at the time of the National People's Congress in March 2003 that all interconnection problems between operators suddenly disappeared—everyone could call through to everyone else. The improvement occurred because operators did not wish to bring upon themselves unwelcome scrutiny. However, this official believed, once the congress dispersed, interconnection problems would arise again.[39]

The basis for interconnection prices in China are the tariff rates—the retail rates consumers pay for services—which are set by the government. As described by a knowledgeable Chinese analyst, tariff rates are based on a combination of factors: market conditions, costs of the operators, and income level of the consumers. Although in principle the State Planning Commission (SPC) is responsible for setting these rates, the SPC has only three employees for price setting in three industries—telecom, airline, and rails.[40] Therefore, as a practical matter, say MII officials, the ministry can decide small changes in tariff rates, but larger changes are submitted by MII to the SPC for approval.[41] Tariff setting will be discussed in greater detail in Chapter 7.

The Chinese government has only begun to establish a procedure for more systematic accounting of state-owned enterprise costs, including those of the telecommunications operators. At a general level, the establishment of the SPC in 2003 resulted in regular reporting of state-owned enterprise accounts at the national level. In a similar vein, MII had earlier adopted, in 2002, a new accounting system that requires operators to provide cost data on an annual basis. MII Minister Wu Ji-chuan's early 2003 major work meeting of the ministry called for better resolution of interconnection issues. According to one of the officials involved, this effort includes a project to develop an economic cost model to establish interconnection rates. This represents a departure from the practice of setting interconnection rates based on retail tariff rates. The development of a cost model would involve the collection of detailed information from operators. The challenge, however, will be both to extract relevant data from the operators and, once the model is established, to persuade the operators to accept it.[42]

In spite of all of MII's work since its establishment in 1999, the history of the telecommunications ministry in interconnection is mixed. As MPT, the ministry was clearly biased against Unicom and through inaction supported China Telecom's efforts to block Unicom's growth. Since its transformation into MII, the ministry has had some successes, such as the issuance of provisional regulations in 1999, which marked a significant improvement in Unicom's ability to provide the services it was actually licensed to provide in 1993. Yet, despite some achievements, MII is not the final arbiter of interconnection disputes. Tellingly, when Unicom's CDMA dispute arose with China Mobile, it avoided seeking redress with MII and its local communications administration. After failing to get redress from the court, it raised its appeal directly to the State Council.

When asked why operators appealed their local disputes directly to the State Council, one close observer and interconnection expert remarked that as the representative of the government as owner of all the telecommunications operators, a State Council decision was considered the final appeal.[43] Indeed, looking back at the short history of interconnection in China, when Unicom was founded, it was the State Council that put the SPC in charge of resolving the first interconnection dispute. It was the State Council's decision to take drastic action to split China Telecom and MPT in 1999 and to split China Telecom into northern and southern units in 2002. In the spring of 2002, it was the State Council that lent MII weight to resolve the dispute between Unicom's

CDMA service and China Mobile. Furthermore, in early 2003, when MII called for operators to take concerted action to improve the interconnection regime, it was taken seriously because MII was responding to direct demands from the State Council.

Global Context: Interconnection and the WTO

In many telecommunications markets with competition, interconnection long has been a core issue for policymakers and regulators. As the WTO concluded its Agreement on Basic Telecommunications in 1997, however, international telecommunications organizations clarified the global consensus on what constitutes a solid interconnection regime. In the WTO reference paper, there is a section devoted to interconnection. Most notably, this text outlines several basic aspects of interconnection, including the fundamental requirement made of major operators to provide interconnection in a timely fashion and with reasonable terms, the importance of cost-based pricing for interconnection, the need to publish interconnection agreements to improve the quality of information available in the market for competitors, and finally the need to have a clear dispute resolution mechanism.

This reference paper was agreed to by WTO members in 1997 and went into effect in 1998. When China acceded to the WTO, this reference paper was included as part of its commitments. Regionally, both the Asia Pacific Economic Cooperation (APEC)[44] and the Comisión Internacional de Telecomunicaciones (CITEL),[45] part of the Organization of American States, have ministerial statements that elaborate on the importance of interconnection policy and expand on the kinds of principles written in the WTO paper.

China has issued some rules that require operators to interconnect and also has established dispute resolution mechanisms that are in concordance with the WTO principles. However, there are other principles toward which China is still working. First, pricing of interconnection rates is not cost oriented. The ministry is working toward developing an accounting system that will better enable it to assess costs and that will make it possible to ascertain the relationship between the cost of providing interconnection service and the rates charged for it. It is common in markets with a longer history of competition, such as Hong

Kong, Japan, Australia, the United States, and many European countries, to require that incumbent operators offer interconnection based on the results of forward-looking economic cost models, a methodology designed to minimize the level of compensation an incumbent receives for historical inefficiencies. China is considering such a model, but the first step will be to establish cost data. One difficulty is that all operators are state-owned and are not required to release their financial data, except in the case of those limited subsidiaries that have some portion of their stock listed on foreign exchanges. Until reform of the state-owned enterprises generally increases the transparency of their financial performance, improving the effectiveness of China's interconnection regime will be difficult.

Interconnection agreements in China are not public, as they are in many other countries. In Japan, NTT publishes an extensive reference interconnection offer that details the prices and technical conditions for interconnection with its network. In the United States, interconnection agreements are published and frequently posted to the Internet by state public utility commissions. In Europe, many regulators have published reference interconnection agreements, and this practice is further outlined in the European Commission Directives related to interconnection and access for electronic communications. The importance of publishing interconnection agreements is that it provides to new entrants some basic information to enable them to make investment and other business decisions. Without this information, new entrants find it difficult to reach reasonable interconnection agreements against dominant operators with market power. In those parts of the telecommunications markets where dominant market power of an incumbent is absent—in the mobile telephony market in some countries, for example—such publication of interconnection agreements is less necessary for competition.

Conclusion

The more competition develops in China's market, the more complex interconnection questions will become. To date, new interconnection problems arise from the entry of new firms into the telecommunications market. A familiar pattern emerges, as described in Figure 6.1. When the Chinese government initially allowed Unicom to enter the market in 1993, no interconnection regime existed. Unlike some ideas,

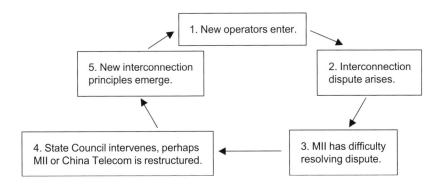

FIGURE 6.1   Patterns in interconnection policy

such as the general notion that competition in telecommunications would help the country's development, the technical theory and practice of interconnection in other parts of the world had little impact in China. The most significant interconnection actions the government has taken are the twice structural separation of China Telecom in 1999 and 2002. While the entry of every new firm created more interconnection problems, the oldest new entrant—Unicom—saw benefits in its interconnection arrangements each time.

Institutionally, the telecommunications ministry has hesitated at every opportunity to take decisive action. At the local level, the provincial and city telecommunications administrations have followed the indecision of MII in Beijing, as personified by MII Minister Wu Jichuan. Instead, the State Council has been responsible for settling the most difficult interconnection disputes. In the State Council, then Premier Zhu Rongji and Vice Premier Wu Bangguo appear to have taken the most visible roles.

An ill-functioning interconnection regime can devastate competition in the telecommunications market in favor of the incumbent operators, and the consequences are immediately perceived by consumers. The quick desertion by Unicom's CDMA customers in Nanyang, Henan Province, is a good example. Although the marketing and value of the service attracted substantial numbers of subscribers, the poor quality of the service, in large part due to lack of good interconnection arrangements with Nanyang Mobile, caused nearly half the subscribers to leave Unicom within a year. MII's weakness leaves a vacuum filled by the most powerful telecommunications firms and fiats from the State Council. Until the MII fully commits to competition, can access cost data from the operators, and develops a firm grasp of the regulatory tools to determine interconnection pricing, the regulatory regime's weaknesses will continue, and telephone service quality in China will suffer.

7 Chasing the Consumer
Retail Pricing of Telecommunications in China

Extracting money from city dwellers or businesses to subsidize telecommunications service for country dwellers or residential households, respectively, is quite a common policy approach in telecom. To achieve social objectives, such as promoting telecommunications in underserved areas, governments frequently regulate retail prices. The Chinese government also built such subsidies into the pricing regime. However, by allowing competition, the market put downward pressure on prices and began to squeeze dry the source of the subsidy. On top of this, to meet the overwhelming demand of consumers, Chinese operators routinely flout the state's authority and set prices lower than those established by the government guidelines. In the face of this reality, the government has stated that it will eventually abolish price controls for telecommunications service.

In telecommunications, tariffs are the schedule of rates and regulations governing the provision of telecommunications services by a particular carrier.[1] In this chapter, the focus is on the retail rates set by the government to govern the prices consumers pay for telecommunications services. In highly regulated regimes, governments decide the tariff rates, and once these rates are published, operators are required to adhere to them. A variety of methods can be used to develop rates. There is an extensive economic literature on rate making that discusses how to assess cost data and build economic models to set rates that achieve a preordained policy objective.[2] The objective can range from maximizing investment in the telecommunications network to stimulating demand for telecommunications services. In some deregulated markets, operators submit changes to tariffs to the government, and these changes go into effect either with government approval or, in some regimes, automatically without government review. In the most liberal regimes, retail rates are no longer bound by tariffs. In these regimes, the government no longer sets rates, and operators are free to set rates at market levels in negotiation with their customers—essentially like any other service from car repair to the restaurant business.

In developing countries, the government commonly sets tariffs to stimulate demand for telecommunications service. Operating on the hypothesis that people with little income will use only telecommunications services that are cheap, rates for local calls are frequently set at a very low level, often below the cost of providing the service. Local service is subsidized by other services, often by rates charged for domestic or international long distance or by services used by other groups, such as businesses. This kind of cross-subsidization is easy to implement when there is a monopoly operator but difficult to sustain in a multioperator competitive market. In a multioperator competitive market, to maintain below-cost rates for local telephony and very high above-cost rates for long distance is to create incentives for companies to exit the local telephony service market and to enter the long distance telephony market. The challenge of reforming tariffs to better reflect the cost of providing service is commonly referred to as the need to "rebalance tariffs." Tariffs that are not "balanced," relative to the underlying cost of providing the service, create distortions in the market.

Therefore, as a telecommunications market transitions from a single operator to multioperator competitive environment, tariffs need to be rebalanced in order to prevent distortions in the market. If tariffs for long distance and international service are very high, this serves as an incentive for companies to invest more in this area. The same is true in reverse if tariffs for local service are too low. Frequently in developing countries, telecommunications service is scarce not because there is no demand; instead, because tariffs for local telecommunications service are low, there is in fact an excess demand for the service but a disincentive for the operator to invest capital to supply the service. Also, there is some evidence that low-income households are willing to spend more of their income on telephone service than previously expected, suggesting that government policy should set prices designed to increase investment and supply of services rather than prices designed to stimulate demand.[3]

Rebalancing tariffs, however, is very difficult politically. Citizens accustomed to low local telephony rates usually are not aware that the rates are below the cost of providing the service and are often enraged at the suggestion they be raised. Similarly, in many societies where long distance service is used by the affluent, lowering these rates appears to be a perk to the rich just as the poor are being squeezed for higher local rates. The irony is that if rebalancing does not occur, the likely long-term consequence is a decline in the investment necessary to provide local service and a deterioration in the quality of the service, a severely disturbing consequence in countries that as of yet do not have extensive networks.

China's Tariff Policy Framework

Although most prices in the Chinese economy are no longer set by the central government, telecommunications service is one of the few exceptions. The government organizations involved in tariff setting are the MII and the State Planning and Development Commission (SPDC), before 1998 known as the State Planning Commission. Pricing policies in general are the responsibility of the SPDC. However, as one observer noted, the SPDC has three officials to cover three industries: telecommunications, airlines, and railways.[4] According to MII officials, most of the tariff setting work and minor tariff changes, therefore, are undertaken by the MII. Major tariff changes are submitted by the MII to the SPDC for approval.[5] Other government players include the local telecommunications authorities who have a key role in setting some retail rates. Local offices will submit tariff rates for the local SPDC offices to approve. For such services as calls within a city, the SPDC and MII will have guidelines, but local telecommunication administrations will set the prices.[6] These locally set tariffs appear sometimes to conform and sometimes not to conform to national rules.

As discussed in Chapter 4, all the major telecommunications operators are state-owned enterprises. Their financial data are not published, except for those parts of operators that have been listed on the Hong Kong and U.S. stock exchanges. When asked, the companies pledge that their main objective is profits. However, their largest stockholder is ultimately the state, and typically, the goal of state bureaucracies is to maximize size—in the case of telecommunications, usually the number of subscribers—even if growing larger is an apparent drain on profitability. During the 1990s, operators consistently invented ways of setting market prices for their services that clearly were below the government tariff rates. It is possible that this is profit-maximizing behavior. It is also possible that this is behavior pursuing objectives that are not profit maximizing.

In China, there are two categories of telecommunications service: basic and nonbasic. Basic services are used widely and include local wireline, long distance wireline, and mobile phone rates. The government sets tariffs for basic services. Nonbasic services are often new services. Typically, there are government guidelines only for nonbasic service rates, or there is no guidance at all. For the basic services, there are three ways of setting the tariffs. First, the government can allow service prices to be set simply by the market. Operators set these rates according to market demand and report them to the government, which discourages operators from setting rates that are lower than costs, a primary concern of the government as it owns all these operators. The second option is that the government sets guidelines. The SPDC, MII, and the local telecommunications administration jointly develop the guidelines. These take the form of a standard national price guideline and a specified margin to give flexibility to localities. The third option is that the government develops a national price standard. SPDC and MII set the national standard, with a specified margin that gives the local administration some flexibility in implementation. The price standard is less flexible than a price guideline.[7]

Tariff guidelines and national standards always include a specified percentage margin above and below the rate so as to offer local telecommunications administrations some flexibility in adapting the national rule to local conditions.[8] Incumbent operators such as China Mobile and China Telecom do not enjoy any legal flexibility. However, nonincumbent carriers do. The other operators can set their prices within 10 percent of the rate. Usually, they opt to set prices 10 percent below the rate.

The following sections discuss the history of tariffs for wireline and mobile services in the 1990s. They document the government's meticulous efforts to control pricing in telecommunications in the midst of scattered efforts by operators to adapt to market demands. For most countries, tariff setting places a ceiling on local telephony prices and a price floor on long distance and international services. In China, as in other countries, the government has unsuccessfully tried through tariffs to set a price floor on long distance and international services. However, in the area of local service, over the 1990s it became clear that the tariff setting exercise is also an effort to maintain a price floor, not a price ceiling. As new technologies and other innovations created downward pressure on telecommunication service prices, the telecommunications ministry has repeatedly intervened in an effort to maintain the minimum tariff level. The government is concerned that price wars are "bad competition" and has consistently tried to prop up prices.

The Rise and Fall of Installation Fees

In the early 1990s, MPT resisted rebalancing tariffs. Hong Kong scholar John Ure noted in 1994:

> Although the MPT and the Government of China has been strongly advised by the World Bank to apply the general price reforms of recent years to the telecommunications sector, fears of risking political unpopularity and even social unrest at a time when the rate of inflation in many cities is 20 or 30 percent have compelled them to hold off. An additional explanation is the inertia frequently associated with the Ministry, and underlying this is the reality that in China, as anywhere else there are conservative and reformist elements in all organizations and in all walks of life. Without a strong external challenge, such as competition from a new entrant, or a strong political directive from the State Council level, the nature of bureaucracy is to prolong decision making in the name of "consensus" or simply to put things on indefinite hold.[9]

The process for changing tariffs in China at this time was for the telecommunications ministry to propose changes for approval by the

SPDC of the State Council. In the early 1990s, a scattered menu of tariffs were merged into three main ones: a one-time installation fee for wireline service or a network connection fee for wireless, a flat monthly fee, and a schedule of per-minute fees based on usage and varying by service—local, domestic long distance, Hong Kong/Taiwan/Macau long distance, and international long distance.

In the early 1990s, getting a telephone subscription was expensive not because the charges for domestic service were high but because the installation fee for a wireline phone, or the comparable network connection fee for a wireless phone, was several times the average monthly income of most Chinese. Usage fees for international service were high, but domestic service fees were low. The high installation charges in the early days meant that few households could afford a telephone line themselves and that most residential phones were provided by work units. Furthermore, the high installation cost meant that many telephone handsets were attached to a single main line, leading to high network congestion, with some provinces reporting call completion rates of 30 percent or less.[10]

In the early 1990s, the SPDC and the MPT deliberately established very high installation and network connection rates in order to generate capital that would enable the rapid deployment of the telecommunications network during the mid-1990s. Although it was a policy that generated investment in network expansion, it also generated much consumer complaint. Adding fuel to consumers' irritation was the fact that for fixed line accounts not only was the installation fee high, but also the waiting period could be well over a month. Figures 7.1 and 7.2 show the changes in the official installation and network connection fees over the last several years.

Although complete statistics are not available, it appears that the period of highest installation and connection fees occurred in the early 1990s. The peak rate was about 5000 yuan (US$600)—for a wireless subscription in 1992 or a wireline subscription in 1994. Past these peaks, however, there was a clear trend toward lower installation and connection fees. Especially in 1999, there were a significant number of tariff adjustments, which led to a sharp drop in official installation and connection fee levels. In a major development, on December 29 and 30,

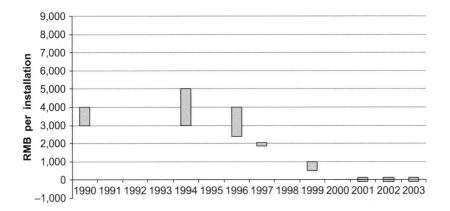

FIGURE 7.1   Wireline installation fees
SOURCES: John Ure, "China's Telecommunications"; Mukil Munish, "China Telecom Slashes Fees"; *China Daily*, "China to Build IP Network"; Xinhua, "China Cuts Mobile Phone Fees"; Chen Zhiming, "Information Ministry Says Telecom Rate Adjustments Expected Soon"; Xinhua, "China Mobile Announces Reduction in Digital Line Leasing, Calling Charges"; Xinhua, "China Unicom to Cut Telephone Fees"; Zhao Huanxin, "Phone Rates Reduction May Trigger Price War"; Xinhua, "China Cancels Telephone Installation Charges"; Interview with government official conducted by author, April 2002, China; Interview with government official conducted by author, June 2002, China; International Telecommunications Union, *ITU World Indicators 2003*

1999, the MII and the SPDC held a joint hearing on lowering telecommunications fees for leased telephone lines and international telephone calls and increasing fees for local calls and postal services. This was MII's first public hearing. In attendance were about fifty participants, including users, operators, representatives from government institutes, nongovernment organizations, and provincial telecommunications administrations, and other experts.[11] By 2001, both the network connection and installation fees had reached zero. This major readjustment of tariff levels, an undertaking that the telecommunications ministry was so unwilling to take five years earlier, was driven partly by market changes and partly by political pressure. While official fee levels remained high, consumers flocked to service packages that offered illegal discounts. Both legal and illegal operators offered service packages at unofficial prices.

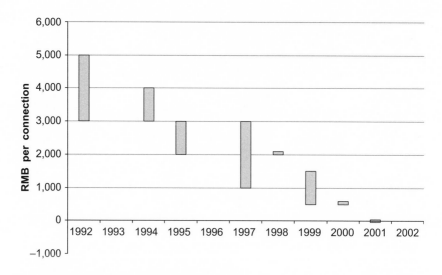

FIGURE 7.2 Wireless network connection fees
SOURCES: John Ure, "China's Telecommunications"; Mukil Munish, "China Telecom
Slashes Fees"; *China Daily*, "China to Build IP Network"; Xinhua, "China Cuts Mobile
Phone Fees"; Chen Zhiming, "Information Ministry Says Telecom Rate Adjustments
Expected Soon"; Xinhua, "China Mobile Announces Reduction in Digital Line Leasing,
Calling Charges"; Xinhua, "China Unicom to Cut Telephone Fees"; Zhao Huanxin,
"Phone Rates Reduction May Trigger Price War"; Xinhua, "China Cancels Telephone
Installation Charges"; Interview with government official conducted by author, April
2002, China; Interview with government official conducted by author, June 2002,
China; International Telecommunications Union, *ITU World Indicators 2003*

Price Wars in Mobile Service

While the MII, SPDC, and local telecommunications administrations labored through the process of tariff reforms, particularly in
the mobile phone sector, operators openly flouted government standards. Especially starting in late 1998 and all through 1999, there was a
steady stream of media reports on illegal price wars occurring in the
cellular service market that were driving prices well below the government tariffs. The *Hong Kong Standard* reported that starting in January 1999, in Guangdong Province, China Telecom's monthly fees for
mobile service would be cut by 50 percent, to 50 yuan (US$6.25). A
few months earlier, Unicom's Guangdong operation had also cut its
basic monthly fee to 50 yuan (US$6.25)—thus, China Telecom's ac-

tion appeared to match its rival's cut exactly. Although the cut reduced revenue from monthly fees, China Telecom hoped for an increase in cellular use, the *Hong Kong Standard* reported. These cuts in cellular rates made using a mobile phone cheaper than using a wireline phone.[12]

In April 1999, Unicom started offering a mobile service known as "city card service." The connection fee was 200 yuan (US$24), 60 percent of the 500 yuan (US$60) tariff; the monthly rate was 20 yuan (US$2.4), 40 percent of the 50 yuan (US$6) tariff; and the usage rate was 0.2 yuan (US$0.02) per minute, half the 0.4 yuan (US$0.05) per-minute tariff. In January 2000, China Mobile offered the "Shenzhou OK" card, which required only a usage fee of 0.6 RMB (US$0.07) per minute and no connection or monthly fee—a price structure not permitted by the official tariff (see Figures 7.3 and 7.4).[13]

In May 1999, MII announced a crackdown on illegal discounts on mobile phone fees, especially as China Mobile's illegal discounts were endangering Unicom's financial health.[14] However, Unicom did not escape unscathed. The media reported that the Hubei Provincial Price Bureau implemented central government policy by cracking down on China Unicom's mobile service charges cut. It was noted that Unicom

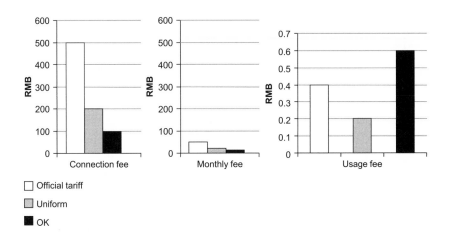

□ Official tariff

▨ Uniform

■ OK

FIGURE 7.3 Price competition in connection, monthly fees, and usage: Official tariff vs. Unicom vs. Shenzhou OK card, January 2000
SOURCE: Zhang Xinzhu, *Zhongguo Jichu Sheshi Chanye*

also transgressed regulations in Wuhan, where its branch was offering packages with no connection fees and local call rates that were half the national standards.[15]

The director of the Telecommunications Administration Bureau of MII publicly reaffirmed in November 1999 the policy that prices for mobile telecommunications services are set by the state and that mobile operators cannot change them. Unicom and China Mobile are both responsible for "increasing state assets," said MII, and unauthorized rate changes not only harm each business but also cause losses to the state. Some operators' local branches had offered packages that waived connection fees and provided free usage time. They were not allowed to do so and were required to report to their headquarters and MII for approval, according to MII. The companies were also required to establish a hotline for consumers to complain or report illegal activities. MII also announced that tariffs would be reviewed shortly thereafter.[16]

With only two rivals in the mobile market, it is difficult to explain why China would experience price wars. In most mobile telephony markets with only two operators, the duopoly is an environment conducive to collusion. In other words, each operator seeks to maintain the highest possible rates for consumers, and no one operator is willing to disturb this highly lucrative position for the other. In fact, in the United States, there was a policy of duopoly adopted for cellular service in the 1980s—the stickiness of high prices was one reason that more licenses were eventually issued in the market, a policy shift that did decrease prices. Are Chinese duopolists different? Perhaps they are because they are state owned. The MII's November 1999 statement gives a clue—by reiterating that the operators are government assets, the statement implies that the operators would not be permitted to lose money for the government by offering services at rates that are too low. State-owned enterprises are not always profit-seeking firms. They have other goals that are more similar to those of government bureaucracies—such as expanding the number of staff or increasing the size of their budgets. Seeking more subscribers would certainly accomplish these objectives and could be the incentive that drove duopolists to price wars in China's mobile telecommunications market.

New Technologies Challenge Tariffs Further

In addition to the fundamental issue of operator ownership, which created incentives for operators to subvert tariffs, the emergence of new technologies to provide voice telephony that were not tariffed services created arbitrage opportunities for entrepreneurs all over the country. The emergence of every new technology provoked an attempt by MII to stamp out the new technology. How hard the MII would try to stop a new technology and whether MII would be successful depended largely on the political clout of the operators involved.

Around 1997, IP telephony service emerged, enabling voice telecommunications over the Internet rather than over the traditional telecommunications network. The details of how this service emerged are discussed in the next chapter. Essentially, the service enabled individual entrepreneurs—sometime with no more than a single desktop computer—to offer domestic and international telecommunications services at a fraction of the official tariff. Demand for the service grew so rapidly that local telecommunications offices were compelled to take action against these entrepreneurs. By 1999, MII had legalized Voice over Internet Protocol (VOIP) and set a tariff for the service equal to the market price. It is also well known in the market that the major telecommunications operators were marketing the excess capacity of the traditional telecommunications network as VOIP, flouting both the traditional telecommunications tariff and the IP tariff. By 2000, the government had stopped setting VOIP tariffs all together. Although the quality of VOIP is sometimes slightly inferior, it is a good substitute for traditional long distance, and it dramatically reduced major operators' revenue for all traditional domestic and international long distance.

In April 1999, an article in *China Daily* on tariff developments of the previous year suggested that illegal experimentation with other price structures and other technologies, such as cable television, could prove lucrative. Whereas in Beijing at this time the fee for installing a telephone ran to about 1000 yuan (US$125), with a waiting period of two months, some local radio and television offices in Leshan, in Sichuan Province, and Zibo, in Shandong Province, were offering telephone service over their cable television networks. They charged no installation fee and a

monthly fee of less than 50 yuan (US$6) for unlimited use. China Tele-
com asked local governments to ban them as illegal businesses.[17] These
incidents demonstrate the possibility of the cable networks entering as
competitors in the telecommunications industry, despite the fact that
their legal status was unclear. As discussed in Chapter 3, although MII
was apparently willing to open the telecommunications market to broadcasters, the relevant broadcasting authorities—protected by the powerful Communist Party propaganda system—were not willing to open
their media market to telecommunications operators.

In the meantime, Little Smart, a different kind of wireless telephony service—not as powerful or as convenient as cellular service but nevertheless offering reasonable service within a limited geographic area—was
introduced at the end of 2000 by China Telecom. Little Smart is a wireless
telecommunications service that has only very basic functions, has virtually no roaming area, and does not work during high-speed travel. However, a three-minute call costs only 0.20 yuan (US$0.03), one sixth the
average of other wireless phones. Also, the Little Smart system utilizes a
calling-party-pays scheme, different from the mobile-party-pays scheme
allowed by MII and preferred by some consumers. The emergence of this
service is discussed more extensively in the next chapter. China Telecom
introduced this popular service in sixty cities and had about one million
subscribers in 2000. However, the telecom ministry issued four administrative orders to crush the service, one of which tripled the service fees to
stem competition. These steps were taken in spite of at least one official
editorial that made the following argument: "since incomes vary greatly
across the country, the market for mobile telecommunication services is
naturally segmented. Services with differentiated prices can better meet
diversifying user needs for mobile communications." Among government
departments, some disagreed with MII's actions.[18]

In the case of VOIP and Little Smart, when the operators involved were major telecommunications operators the MII and the government eventually accepted the technology as legal. In the case of cable
television operators offering telecommunications services, China Telecom was directly threatened, and these companies had more difficulty
getting started in the market. However, all these cases reveal a willingness of certain firms to offer telecommunications services at prices below the tariffed rate, which suggests either that the tariffs are well above

operators' costs or that these state-owned firms are pursuing market share over profitability.

Tariff Rebalancing in Earnest

The cycle of discounts, official crackdowns, and tariff adjustments continued in 2000. In response to the tariff review cycle of the previous year, beginning in January 2000 China Mobile officially was able to cut its rates from 0.8 yuan (US$0.10) to 0.6 yuan (US$0.0.08) per minute in order to attract more subscribers. However, at this time, China Mobile also introduced pre-paid calling cards for mobile users,[19] which were declared illegal by MII five months later. For the consumers, therefore, the cards stopped working four months before their advertised expiration date. At least one editorial called for the company to be punished for inconveniencing consumers so much: "Price discounts should be one of the main ways to attract customers and win back market share, but it should not be used to defraud customers."[20]

In the immediate aftermath of these problems, consumers became wary of discount offers. An August 2000, a *China Daily* report said that "following a move to give discounts to long-distance callers, the Chongqing branch of China Unicom recently announced it would lower its fees for mobile telephones. Although this appears more good news for the city's mobile telephone users who complained of high prices, the major customers are not yet celebrating. This is because customers do not know whether the announcement will be postponed by top authorities because of regulations like the previous move."[21]

Political pressure on MII was public. "After the premier's famous announcement during an interview that prices of telecommunications services must be significantly reduced," Xinhua reported, further tariff adjustments were discussed at a hearing held by MII and the SPDC in Beijing in September 2000. Official newspaper *China Daily* mocked the hearing as a mere showpiece because of its lack of clarity, although the paper conceded, at least, that the government had shown its willingness to listen to opinions from ordinary consumers.[22] Subsequently, in November 2000, MII announced that a tariff adjustment would be implemented once it obtained State Council approval. In December 2000, the State Council approved a new tariff scheme, the "Notice on Structural

Adjustment of Telecommunications Tariffs," which lowered tariffs, sim-
plified billing schemes, and lowered rates for rural areas.[23] The notice
also rescinded tariffs for paging, VOIP, collocation, and value-added
telecommunications services, allowing firms to set prices freely.[24]

Soon after MII's December 2000 announcement, operators began announcing price changes. Local rates were raised, and international and domestic long distance rates were lowered. This reflected
changes in costs and ended the cross-subsidy from long distance to local
service, said MII officials.[25] A few months later, in February 2001,
China Daily reported that 95 percent of 800 consumers surveyed were
happy with the new billing structure despite the fact that only 11 percent would see their telecommunications bills lowered because of a rise
in local call charges.[26] An MII official said in a private interview, however, that there was negative public reaction to this move.[27] On the MII
website, one could find a defensive editorial from *Guangming Ribao*
written by Qian Puqun:

> In the past few years, the government has adjusted several times tele-
> communications tariffs, and the average tariff on the whole has
> declined substantially. This was undertaken to encourage consump-
> tion, [and] promote telecommunications development. However, for
> various reasons, various views in society have disagreed with these
> changes, particularly consumers [who] have different opinions about
> the rise and fall of certain service prices. Some media and users believe
> the adjustments result in an increase in tariffs, others even think that it
> is a big fraud. Therefore, we want to bring forward some information
> about the situation in an effort to help everyone objectively understand
> this question.[28]

The MII was responding to negative public reaction to the rise in
some tariffs.

In a significant shift, in July 2001, MII announced that the one-
time installation/connection fees would be abolished, both for fixed and
mobile operators.[29] Although this news was welcomed by consumers,
some observers questioned its timing. Prior to the 2001 announcement,
competitors were allowed to charge lower connection fees than China
Telecom, thus improving their relative attractiveness to consumers. As
mentioned in Chapter 4, the abolition of these fees led analysts to ques-

tion whether Unicom and the new operator Railcom would be competitive against incumbent operators without this price advantage. Media reports, however, said that Unicom was trying to recoup such an advantage by offering a 10 percent discount on its basic monthly charge of 50 yuan (US$6.25).[30]

On the basis of appearances, the ministry has been struggling to keep tariffs in line with market developments, rather than the other way around. For example, starting in February 2002, government-set prices for phone cards were lifted, and telecommunications service operators could legally set their own prices. MII was responding to public complaint about its past actions.

> While analysts are hailing the stimulus rule, telecom sellers seem disinterested. Few contacted by the *Beijing Times* newspaper said they will adjust their prices because of the new policy. In fact, many card sellers have already been offering under-the-counter cheap prices due to the fierce competition in the market, some industry insiders noted. Many card dealers are resorting to under-the-counter low pricing strategies despite the government's regulation on the card prices.[31]

In a 2002 interview with a provincial communications administration, officials explained that the nationwide tariff for mobile service is 50 yuan (US$6.25) per month, 0.40 yuan (US$0.05) per minute. Outside the official rules, wireless companies were offering different packages, such as a service plan that permitted local calls but no long distance calling. The monthly rate was only 18 or 25 yuan (US$ 2.25 or US$8.3) per month, with a timed rate of 0.20 yuan (US$0.03) per minute, only two thirds the official rate for wireline service. Although this kind of service package falls outside the rules, the provincial communications administration had not taken action against it because officials believed that such a package made telecommunications service more affordable for many of the local citizens.[32]

Setting tariffs is difficult work, a ministry official complained in early 2002. Several government organizations were involved in setting prices, including the Ministry of Finance and the SPDC, which meant that much coordination was required for a decision. In addition, the media, companies, and consumers constantly complained, said officials.[33]

In March 2002, on the sidelines of the National Party Congress meeting in Beijing, Minister Wu Jichuan remarked, "telecom service prices will eventually be determined and adjusted exclusively by the market."[34] In the meantime, the ministry was forced to revise tariffs in a manner that conformed somewhat to prices actually offered in the market, while trying to minimize losses to the state-owned operators.

Conclusion

By the late 1990s, after resistance earlier in the decade, tariff restructuring in China was proceeding apace. After a few short years when operators were permitted to charge high installation fees for new landline subscriptions and high network connection fees for new wireless subscriptions, the government bowed to market pressure to lower and abolish these fees. Usage fees for various services also shifted—very low local service fees rose, and very high long distance and international service fees fell. The government tried to preserve state-owned operators' revenue by slowing the decline of long distance and international service fees but was unsuccessful against the combined force of operators seeking more subscribers and consumers seeking better prices. Figure 7.4 illustrates a typical cycle of tariff adjustments since 1998. As even newer technologies and the number of operators in the Chinese market expand, it seems reasonable to expect that the government's struggle with tariffs will continue.

The story of tariff reform in China's telecommunications market illustrates the futility of the government's effort to contain the market under state control. In those areas of telecommunications policy where actors are few—such as in decisions on how many operators should be licensed in the market or interconnection, where the only actors are the limited number of operators—the government has more tools available to it to guide the market. In the area of tariffs, where dozens of local branch operators can surreptitiously offer many varieties of service packages to millions of consumers, the state is helpless to guide the market. Consumers and producers of telecommunications services are forcing on the government an ideological shift from command economy pricing to market pricing. However, the fact that all the major opera-

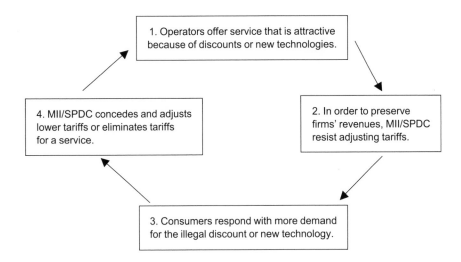

FIGURE 7.4   Patterns in tariff policy

tors continue to be state owned leaves open a question as to whether operators' strategies of tariff evasion and continual discounting are profit-maximizing or simply transfers from the coffers of the state directly into the pockets of consumers.

8   The Triumphant Consumer?

*The Growth of Voice Over Internet Protocol
(VOIP) and "Little Smart" Personal Handyphone Service*

Although the government of the People's Republic of China remains firmly authoritarian, at least in two instances the spark of technological innovation and the power of consumer choice has forced it to
reverse course. These two cases are VOIP, which offers consumers an
opportunity to make cheap long distance calls both domestically and
internationally, and "Little Smart" *(xiao ling tong)*, a new take on an
old technology, which makes mobile phone service more affordable to
the masses. Both these innovations threatened the revenues of important
state-owned telecom operators. Both were banned in the early days following their appearance in the market, although the services were widely
available in the market illegally. Consumers welcomed both services,
and in the end, their numbers were so large that maintaining the prohibi-
tion was untenable. In the face of widespread flouting of its rules, the telecom ministry in each instance reversed stance and legalized the service.

VOIP and Little Smart did face a longer and more protracted
struggle in China than in other countries, and they illustrate the bargaining that takes place among MII and other government organizations responsible for overall economic development. The ministry
maintains a balance of interests among government and state-owned
operators, a kind of state-industry framework, by initially ignoring new
technologies, banning them when they become threats, and co-opting
them when the ban becomes unenforceable. In contrast, other govern-

ment bodies with a broader remit of overall economic development publicly supported these new technologies. Economists who study China find frequently that when the government breaks opens a monopoly, a cycle begins: a free market price competes with a state-controlled price, and there is new entry into the market, more price flexibility, and incremental managerial reforms.[1] Technological change makes it possible for new firms to enter the market.

In addition to technological change, consumer choice was also a major force in the cases of VOIP and Little Smart. Consumers voted with their pocketbooks and supported the new firms that entered the market. For both VOIP and Little Smart, technological change affected prices in the market, and consumers responded to the changes in service price and quality; this response disrupted the state-industry framework and forced the state to repair the framework.

VOIP Challenges Long Distance Services

VOIP is distinguished from traditional telephony in the transmission technique used to carry a call from the originator to the recipient. Traditional telephony, also known as circuit-switched telephony, involves a technology that occupies a definite amount of capacity on a telecommunications network during the entirety of a telephone call. In traditional voice telephony, a call from person A to person B occupies telephone lines between them that are solely dedicated for the duration of that call. Take, for example, an analogous situation from the transportation field. A train is set on railroad tracks between point A and point B. Only one train can travel back and forth at a time. In VOIP, the network is structured differently so that many telephone calls or even other communications, such as e-mail, can share the same capacity of the network at the same time. There is no dedicated capacity between caller A and receiver B during the time of their telephone conversation. A message, whether a voice call or an e-mail, is broken into small units called packets. The packets are labeled and sent into the network, by which each packet is delivered on its own to the final destination. At the destination, the packets are reassembled and delivered to the recipient. Consider another analogous situation posed by the transportation field: a large shipment delivered by a fleet of trucks along a highway system.

Many vehicles can simultaneously use the highway to travel from many points to many other points, but a single shipment can be broken up, dispersed, and reassembled on arrival.[2]

The advantage of VOIP is that it uses network capacity more efficiently than does traditional telephony. Many more telephone calls can be packeted and dumped into the network at the same time. Although improving, VOIP is sometimes of inferior quality to traditional circuit-switched telephony. There is a downside to traditional telephony, too: once circuits are tied up, there is no more capacity for additional calls.

VOIP is often offered at a cheaper price than traditional circuit-switched telephony. The reasons are many. Certain key components differ in an IP network from a traditional network, and as mentioned before, capacity is used more efficiently. However, another reason VOIP is cheaper is that traditional telephony rates are often set above market levels by government rules. Simply because it does not conform to regulatory categories, then, IP falls outside traditional tariff schedules and is offered at a market price. VOIP offers arbitrage opportunities in part because of technical advantages and in part because of the inflexibility of some countries' tariff schemes.

In China, as in other parts of the world, VOIP prices are cheap and consumers love it. "Five free minutes to the USA," read one ad promoting the sale of digital video disc players in the southern province of Fujian. Brothers Chen Yan and Chen Zhui began offering free Internet telephony service to customers in their Internet cafe in October 1997. To provide VOIP service, the Chens legally leased a telecommunications line from the telecommunications carrier and paid for their Internet service. Software made it possible to place voice telephony calls using their Internet subscription. The Chens initially used VOIP just as a promotion, but soon it became a business mainstay. They offered it at a rate of 4.8 yuan (US$0.58) per minute for international calls, about a quarter of the government-mandated tariff of 18 yuan (US$2.17) per minute.[3]

VOIP disrupts the state-industry framework. By launching a commercial service, the Chens were competing directly with China Telecom. China Telecom soon complained that the Chens' service was below the official price, of poor quality, and illegal. In January 1998, China Telecom had the local police arrest the two brothers, confiscate their equipment, and charge them with endangering national security.[4] The Chens were fined 50,000 yuan (US$6024) and one computer. They fought back, demanding redress and arguing that no crime had been committed. In July 1998, the district court decided in favor of the local public security office and China Telecom. The Chen brothers then took their case to a higher court. In November 1998, the Fuzhou mid-level court sought expert opinion on the difference between Internet and traditional telephony.[5] Two months and much media coverage later, Xu Yongdong, judge at the Fuzhou Intermediate People's Court, found in favor of the Chens and ruled that VOIP was a different technology from traditional wireline telephone services.[6] VOIP was found to be just one of many computer information services, which, according to a State Council circular issued in 1993, was not included in China Telecom's legal monopoly; thus, it was a victory for the Chens.[7] The case then returned to the local Mawei court for another review.[8]

Immediately, MII responded to the situation and announced that the VOIP and fax services market would not be liberalized. "If this is allowed to continue unchecked, the consequences are unimaginable," a spokesman for MII said, referring to a possible burgeoning of privately run Internet telephony services all over China.[9] In January 1999, Zhang Chunjiang, director of MII's telecommunications administration bureau, said that Internet telephony damaged the country and the telecom industry's interests and was "tantamount to information smuggling by bypassing government supervisions in our country . . . We will crack down very harshly on these incidents."[10] MII's reaction stemmed partly from the recognition that many small entrepreneurs had secretly been operating VOIP businesses. Around this time, in Zhejiang Province, Qingtian County, the local telecommunications office also had shut down various privately run VOIP businesses for the crime of making excessive profits. The Chens' enterprise was not a singular case but only one in a tide.[11]

In 1999, the local court in Mawei reviewed the case again and, after six months, found the Chen brothers guilty of illegal telecommunications services. Late in 1999, the Fuzhou mid-level court once again reversed the local court's decision. As Professor Zhou Qiren of Beijing University noted, "The Chens have sacrificed 50,000 yuan [US$6024], their computer (almost the entirety of their capital), and two years' worth of work—is this what they get for being pioneers? Those interested in high technology change or innovation in China—see the Chens' case as a warning."[12]

To repair the state-industry framework, instead of liberalizing MII announced that "a strict permit-issuing system will be implemented when conditions are ripe." MII planned to have VOIP administered by a centralized state telecommunications department. MII officials announced that IP phone licensees would need to submit to an examination of their qualifications by MII to be granted an appropriate permit. In contrast, at this time, a SDPC official, Zhang Dongsheng, publicly acknowledged support of the growth of IP phone service to improve the choices for international callers,[13] an indication that within the government there were conflicting views on the benefits of VOIP. The Chinese media presented the Chens as heroes against an MII that was interested only in protecting government revenues, despite the fact that the popularity of VOIP had been driven by widespread dissatisfaction with high telecom prices.[14]

By March 1999, three months after the Fuzhou Intermediate Court's initial decision in favor of the Chen brothers, MII announced that three operators—China Telecom, Unicom, and Jitong—would be allowed to legally offer VOIP on a trial basis. The operators would be required to charge prices identical to the prices the Chens and other entrepreneurs were charging at the time. MII Bureau of Telecommunications Administration Deputy Director Zhou Baoxin said that the government would crack down on other illegal VOIP operators.[15]

Trial services began in May 1999. To make an IP telephone call, users had to buy an IP telephone card, dial an access number unique to each operator, and enter an account number and password.[16] On May 18, Jitong began selling phone card in values of 50, 100, 200, and 500 yuan in twenty-five cities. In less than two days, Jitong received requests for 10,000 cards and had difficulty keeping up with demand.[17] China Telecom began trials in twenty-five major cities with international service to sixteen countries and regions.[18] By June 1999, China Unicom had begun offering IP phone service in twelve cities.[19] In early 2000, when the success of the trials was clear, a debate ensued over how many licenses should be issued. In the end, because MII viewed VOIP as a basic telecommunications service, the ministry chose to limit licenses to the

six major state-owned operators. No licenses were issued to the entrepreneurs so important in getting the service started.

Today, services that are technically illegal reportedly flourish in
China's telecommunications market. At one level, small operators not
licensed for VOIP, such as computer stores and Internet service providers, are providing services at rates much lower than those of China Telecom. However, as these enterprises are small, they have little impact on
the market and have not been prosecuted with any vigor, according to
one Chinese official who works in the Internet arena.[20] In international
service, some claim that only about 5 percent of China's IP phone calls
traverse the officially licensed VOIP operators. Internet service providers
transmit calls via Intranet to Hong Kong or Taiwan and then carry the
calls internationally through large capacity lines leased from China Telecom. This entirely avoids China's public international gateways.[21]

Confirming this trend was a specific case reported by the Hong
Kong paper the *South China Morning Post*. Xiao Puning of Shanghai
was arrested in March 2002 for routing IP telephone calls between the
United States and Vietnam. Xiao leased lines from Shanghai Telecom
and, using smuggled satellite and other telecommunications equipment
from a U.S.-based partner, could deliver telecommunications services to
U.S. consumers calling Vietnam. Xiao's illegal service generated an estimated 2.3 million yuan (about US$280,000). An investigation was trig-
gered when Shanghai Telecommunications reported to police a sharp
increase in traffic on lines leased by Xiao in 2001. Xiao was found
guilty and given an eleven-year jail sentence.[22] In other countries, of
course, with open and competitive telecommunications markets, such
entrepreneurial efforts would be legal.

Industry experts indicate that within China Telecom's operations, the sales office for leasing high capacity lines operates separately
from its sales office for international telephony, which created an opportunity for competition. Leasing lines, for whatever purpose, benefits
these leasing offices regardless of the impact on the company's international telephony service revenues. Provincial telecommunications officials have the authority to take action against these legally murky
activities but have no incentive to do so.[23]

After China Telecom began offering VOIP service in March
2000, the next month Unicom, Jitong, and Netcom claimed that China

Telecom used unfair tactics to compete in VOIP and manipulate the system. The three companies found bottlenecks in IP card distribution channels.[24] In 2003, MII confirmed that much of what was marketed and sold as "VOIP" in China was not VOIP but in fact traditional circuit-switched telephony. Three years later, a report by the U.S. State Department confirmed that this practice continues.[25] Apparently, the operators offering "VOIP" have ample traditional telecommunications capacity and prefer to use that capacity rather than build new IP capacity. More than just price arbitrage, the emergence of VOIP in China is also a case of regulatory arbitrage—as explained by one Chinese official, operators seek to apply the most advantageous regulatory label to a service, whether the service actually provided technically meets the definition of the regulatory classification. [26]

Another form of VOIP is the service enabled by Skype, a popular Internet application that can be downloaded from the Internet to make voice calls between PCs. With additional applications, calls can be made to phones on the traditional public network. Officially, the Chinese government has prevented Skype from expanding its business from PC-to-PC calls to PC-to-telephone calls by preventing the company from setting up gateways in China.[27] However, it is well known that Skype is easily available to consumers in China over Tom.Com, a popular Chinese language website. Although Tom.Com serves customers in mainland China, it is headquartered in Hong Kong and incorporated in the Cayman Islands.[28] Formally, MII's rules do not extend to Hong Kong. The market there is overseen by the Office of the Telecommunications Authority (OFTA), a regulator with a known reputation for supporting competition and innovative technologies.

In general, the main attraction of VOIP is cheaper prices. Since late 2001, MII has relaxed government-set tariffs, and no longer sets prices for VOIP, but continues to set tariffs for traditional long distance. Figure 8.1 shows how attractive IP long distance prices are. In 2005, VOIP prices for long distance were as much as 57 percent less than traditional long distance rates.

In 2001, an estimated 30–40 percent of long distance service was carried by "VOIP." Official government statistics in 2006 put VOIP at over half of all long distance traffic, measured in minutes.

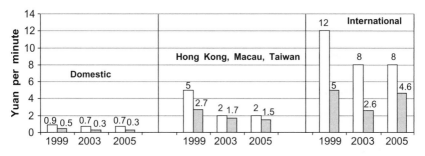

□ Traditional

▣ IP telephony

FIGURE 8.1   Traditional and IP long distance rates
SOURCES: Ministry of Information Industry; Interview with business person conducted by author, March 2003; Michael Wang, "China Internet Protocol Phone Services"; China Telecom; China Netcom

In conclusion, VOIP technology gave new entrants an opportunity to offer cheap telephone service. Beating the official telephone rates was not hard, as they were held artificially high to subsidize other services. These new entrants, however, were outside the government's plan for telecom development. Although the courts and SDPC were not necessarily against the new entrants, in the end MII succeeded in cutting them out of the VOIP business and returning to the status quo state- industry framework. In the main, the benefits of the new technology flow to the major state-owned operators. However, as long as there are still good business opportunities in providing service that is cheaper than the official rates, gray area services flourish using IP and other technologies.

For wireline operators such as China Telecom and China Netcom, most of their revenue historically came from local and long distance service. This massive migration of traffic from one regulatory category to another squeezes domestic and international long distance service market revenues. See Figure 8.2 for a comparison of long distance traffic. Although retail prices for domestic and long distance market are still set by the government, they are doomed in the face of competition from VOIP. With VOIP squeezing this market, wireline operators are driven to seek other sources of revenue.

Long distance: Domestic

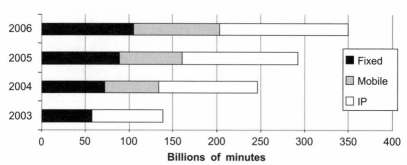

Billions of minutes

Long distance: Hong Kong, Macau, Taiwan

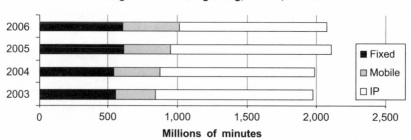

Millions of minutes

Long distance: Other international

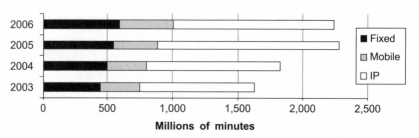

Millions of minutes

FIGURE 8.2 Long distance traffic
SOURCE: Ministry of Information Industry, *Guonei changtu dianhua* and *Guoji gang au tai dianxinye*

Little Smart: Fixed vs. Cellular Operators

For wireline operators, one of these alternative revenue sources is Little Smart, which is like a cellular phone service but usable only within a specific geographic area. Based on personal handyphone service (PHS) technology from Japan, Little Smart has been described as a kind of extended cordless phone service. The core of the network is a wireline network, but the last extension from the network to the consumer is wireless. In telecommunications, this last extension to the customer is known as the local loop, which, on a per customer basis, is usually the most expensive part of the network to build. However, for telecommunications operators that already have wireline networks, the Little Smart technology makes building local loops relatively inexpensive. In China, as of late 2001, the cost of building a wired local loop to a new subscriber was about 1500 yuan (US$180). However, adding a Little Smart subscriber cost China Telecom only 1000 yuan (US$120), and by 2003, the cost had fallen to about 700 yuan (US$84) per subscriber.[29] Although behind the mobile handset, the Little Smart and cellular service networks are different, from the consumer point of view the difference is only a matter of degree. When initially introduced, the Little Smart service could be used only from a limited service area, such as a single city. If the consumer left that city, for example, the phone might not work. However, many consumers who previously could not afford cellular service offered by the wireless operators could afford the wireless local loop service offered by the wireline operators. Priced attractively, these wireless local loop services have grown quickly.

Little Smart and cellular phone price packages vary, but Little Smart is cheaper. Figure 8.3 illustrates some of the government-sanctioned price packages available in 2001, comparing Little Smart with Unicom and China Mobile packages. However, media reports have since indicated that, in contrast to the government-set tariffs, Little Smart usage rates can be as low as 0.2 yuan (US$0.02) for the first three minutes and 0.1 yuan for every minute thereafter.[30]

Beyond lowering the level for usage charges, Little Smart service was also the first to introduce one-way charges in China's wireless telephony market. In China, as in many other markets, such as the United States and Singapore, most cellular phone subscribers pay for

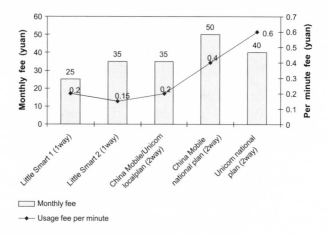

FIGURE 8.3   Cellular and Little Smart prices
SOURCES: Cellular mobile service subscribers: International Telecommunications Union; International Telecommunications Union, "ITU World Indicators 2003"; Little Smart subscribers: AFX News, "China Netcom to Offer Xiaolingtong Service in Beijing Soon"; *Financial Times*, "New Users of China's Little Smart Reaches 10 Million"

both making and receiving phone calls, a system known as two-way charging, receiving-party-pays, or mobile-party-pays. The alternative payment system, popular in markets in Europe and Japan, for example, is a one-way charging system or calling-party-pays. The mobile phone subscriber pays only for outgoing calls; incoming calls are free to the mobile phone subscriber. Instead, the person who originates the call to the mobile phone user usually pays a higher fee.

Consumers in China, accustomed to one-way charging on the wireline network, have long expressed a preference for one-way charging for mobile services. Educated consumers regularly describe the fact that China has a two-way charging system for mobile services as "unreasonable," although by international standards such a pricing scheme is not uncommon. The emergence of Little Smart with a one-way charging system responds to this consumer demand and has intensified the debate in China as to whether the entire mobile regime should be shifted to a one-way charging system. In short, Little Smart's combination of cheaper prices and a one-way charging system is immensely attractive to consumers.

Little Smart began in 1997 as a service approved by the telecom ministry for deployment in rural areas. In 1998, a temporary spectrum frequency allocation was granted to China Telecom. However, as a practical matter, Little Smart service began deployment not in rural areas but in small- and medium-sized cities.[31] In 1999, an order from MII told wireline telecommunications carriers to stop developing Little Smart's PHS. However, China Telecom continued to provide the service. In 2000, MII agreed to recognize Little Smart as legal under two conditions: first, MII insisted that Little Smart not be deployed in large cities, only in smaller cities, recognizing a development that already had taken place; second, MII set a tariff for Little Smart service, which was higher than wireline tariffs but lower than mobile tariffs. Again, China Telecom defied MII public announcements and deployed Little Smart into provincial capitals, which, with populations of three to five million, are considered large cities. MII retreated again and prohibited Little Smart service only in the three largest cities: Beijing, Shanghai, and Guangzhou.

In September 2001, the CEO and chairman of cellular operator Unicom, Yang Xianzu, remarked that he believed that Little Smart was not a threat to Unicom because MII would terminate China Telecom's spectrum rights. That did not happen. Despite Unicom's hopes, MII's attitude to Little Smart actually remained vague. Indecision favored the wireline operators over the cellular operators. At that time, China Telecom was offering Little Smart in about 300 cities, and numbers of Little Smart subscribers sometimes exceeded those of Unicom. In Zhaoqing City, China Telecom's Little Smart subscribership was reported to be 100,000, twice that of Unicom, but only a fraction of China Mobile's 300,000 subscribers.[32] By the end of 2001, Little Smart reportedly had attracted five million users in China. When China Telecom was split into China Telecom and China Netcom, Netcom also sought to grow and expand its Little Smart services.[33]

By early 2002, the cellular operators were expressing concern that in fact Little Smart was placing pressure on the cellular market. China Mobile chairman Wang Xiao Chu said in March 2002, that at the lower price end of its cellular service, Little Smart was a competitor.[34] In July 2002, MII reportedly ordered the halt of Little Smart's introduction into Beijing and Tianjin because of the possible negative impact on China Mobile and China Unicom's share value. Little Smart's entry into the biggest cities—Beijing, Guangzhou, Shanghai—was expected to have the most severe impact on investors' perception of the two cellular carriers. Furthermore, rumors resurfaced at the time that MII might finally issue two new cellular licenses to China Telecom and China Netcom. However, in the summer of 2002, MII Minister Wu said only that two new cellular licenses would be issued in the future but not in the short-term.[35]

In February 2003, the Little Smart dam broke on Beijing, Shanghai, and Guangzhou. As a foreign analyst noted with amusement, "[Little Smart] networks are theoretically verboten everywhere. But, we had thought that they were more verboten in the Tier 1 cities [Beijing, Shanghai, Guangzhou], with Beijing the likely last holdout." In other words, if Little Smart could be offered in Beijing, right under the noses of the national government cadres, without negative repercussions for the operators, the service could be offered anywhere in the country. Trials in Shanghai began at this time as well.[36]

MII struggled, but not mightily, to repair the state-industry framework. The media began to circulate rumors that MII's ban on the service might be rescinded officially.[37] Indeed, on March 12, 2003, MII Minister Wu announced that the government would no longer ban wireline operators from developing Little Smart service in major cities. Specifically, Wu said, MII's policy would be "neither to encourage nor to intervene." *China Daily*, known for expressing official government views, released the following opinion:

> New telecommunications technology can either make or break a monopoly, so the industrial authority should always put consumers first when introducing new businesses. It was reported that on Monday Xiaolingtong, or "Little Smart," a citywide mobile service . . . finally made its way to Beijing—one of the two last forbidden areas designated by the Ministry of Information Industry (MII) for the personal handphone service (PHS) . . . This is long-awaited good news for the consumer as the new system will not only offer them a cheaper telecommunications service, but pressure mobile phone operators to substantially slash their widely criticized high charges . . . Being the industrial authority, however, the MII was understandably worried about the impact of wireless technology if adopted by fixed [wireline] line operators as it may cut too deeply into mobile markets and affect the development of mobile phone

operators. While heeding the interest of mobile phone operators, unfortunately, the industrial watchdog did not listen to the public's deafening cry for lower mobile phone service charges . . . Unstoppable technological progression will only further fuel market competition in a way that regulators and ex-monopoly companies have yet to adapt themselves to. The Xiaolingtong issue is just one test of nerves for them.[38]

Within the month, Little Smart service was available in Beijing. Editorials expressing similar sentiments appeared over the next few weeks in newspapers around the country. Most notable was the opinion released by official news agency Xinhua on April 10, which stated that Little Smart offered improved consumer choice.[39] Given the government's control of the media, the release of such opinions confirms that significant parts of the government supported Little Smart.[40] Observers, such as Yang Peifang, researcher at China Institute of Telecommunications Research, have noted that by delaying for as long as possible its approval for cellular operators to offer discounts to compete with Little Smart, MII actually abetted Little Smart development.[41]

In Guangdong in March 2003, cellular operator Unicom launched a counterattack with a package it called "Unicom Little Smart," which allowed subscribers within designated urban areas to enjoy pricing similar to China Telecom's Little Smart. Outside a designated urban area, charges similar to cellular phone service applied. China Telecom's subsidiary Guangdong Telecom lodged a complaint against Guangdong Unicom's use of the "Little Smart" trade name and argued that its price cuts needed preapproval by government departments.[42] As one analyst put it, while "trying to fend off the Little Smart hordes," China Mobile and Unicom began engaging in "guerilla warfare in the local areas."[43] China Mobile and Unicom offered discounted rates, free minutes, and one-way charging—all things not contemplated in officially sanctioned price packages.

Good subscriber statistics on Little Smart services are difficult to obtain because of the service's murky legal status. However, in 2001, there were reports of five million subscribers; by the end of 2002, there were reports of over ten million subscribers.[44] Based on data released by MII and the operators, Figure 8.4 demonstrates not only that Little Smart subscribership now approaches 100 million, but also that for

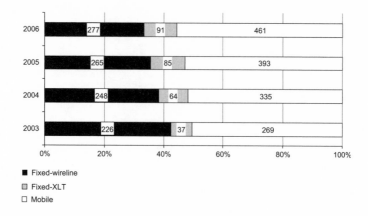

FIGURE 8.4   Total telecom subscribers (in millions)
SOURCE: Ministry of Information Industry, China Netcom, China Telecom, U.S. Securities and Exchange Commission

fixed operators, Little Smart is a source of more rapid subscriber growth than that experienced by traditional fixed service. For the short-term, at least, Little Smart is an increasingly important option for new subscribers to wireless telephony in China. By the end of 2002, there were reports of the service in the three cities where the service was banned.[45] By the end of 2006, there were over ninety million subscribers.

China Telecom and China Netcom, both without cellular telephony licenses and facing the threat of declining revenue from domestic and international long distance service due to competition from VOIP, have sought to provide a kind of mobile service within the spectrum frequency assigned to them by the government. Executives of the operators who were offering Little Smart service claimed that because they already had wireline networks, the additional investment required to deploy Little Smart was small compared with the potential gain. They said that their companies were investing in the Little Smart service because the best opportunities for growth were in mobile services. The fact that these operators were explicitly prohibited from offering cellular service and were not likely to receive licenses for such services until some uncertain time in the future gave them additional incentive to experiment with Little Smart.[46]

Both VOIP and Little Smart are technologies used in different parts of the world. As in China, in many emerging economies VOIP met great resistance from governments seeking to protect the revenues of their incumbent telecom operators, many of which remain monopolies today. However, in most middle and highly developed economies, VOIP has been welcomed as an innovative service that competes on price and quality with existing services. In Japan, VOIP as an adjunct to broadband service dramatically decreased prices for long distance and international calls, a phenomenon welcomed by both consumers and the government. Similar developments are now beginning in North America and Europe. The main question in these markets is not whether to allow VOIP, but whether certain scarce resources, such as telephone numbers, should be allotted to it or whether the service should be connected to emergency networks—for example, the 911 service in the United States.[47]

Similar to Little Smart, technology that depends on wireless local loop systems with mobile handsets is growing in popularity in parts of the world where a significant fraction of the population still do not have easy access to wireline telephones. Other than China, the most prominent example is India, where such "limited mobility" phones quickly doubled the availability of phones nationwide. In contrast to China, India did not ban the limited mobility phones but instead, after an extensive public debate, transformed its licensing regime to treat limited mobility operators equally to cellular and wireline operators. Today, therefore, the legal standing of these limited mobility operators is clear, and companies' investment in these networks is geared toward serving current customers who demand a cheap service and toward future customers who are likely to demand advanced services, such as video and Internet.[48]

Although to observers of the market in China the state's adaptation to VOIP and Little Smart may seem quick, in an international context China is squarely in the company of emerging economies that resist technological change that challenges incumbent operators' main business activities. India's regulatory innovation, for example, in rationalizing licensing regulations for the wireless local loop is a significant example of a government that embraced technology with greater agility than China. China adapts quickly, but in the area of technology, much of the rest of the world is adapting even faster.

Can technology force an authoritarian government to change? Yes, it can, but in the case of VOIP and Little Smart, the change was evolutionary, not revolutionary. China is relatively willing to use state power to slow down innovation if it challenges the established balance of power among government ministries and state-owned enterprises. The cases of VOIP and Little Smart demonstrate that at this stage, the ministry is willing to take decisions to protect its state-industry framework, even though these decisions are unenforceable and, therefore, risk undermining the ministry's credibility. Numerous interviewees indicated that they gave little credence to MII decisions, confirming that the kind of cyclical reform and retrenchment, as illustrated in Figure 8.5, of which VOIP and Little Smart are only two examples, does weaken the standing of the state over time.

The history of VOIP and Little Smart confirms current models of China's political economy. In the area of politics, the tension between MII's interests in preserving the viability of its licensees, the major state-owned operators, and the interests of other state institutions concerned with the overall development of the economy, especially the many entities and individuals who use telecommunications services, is consistent with other studies' views of the Chinese state as fragmented in authority, with different bureaucracies competing and bargaining for power and resources. The novel aspect of these two case studies is that technological

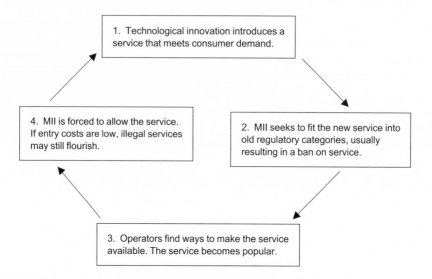

FIGURE 8.5 China's approach toward new technology: Challenge, defense, and retrenchment

change enabled the creation of popular services, which in turn led to recalculations in the relationships between bureaucracies and the relationship between the state and industry. The emergence of VOIP and Little Smart in both instances destabilized the industry structure; in the first case, small-sized entrepreneurs quickly appeared in the market as competitors to China Telecom; in the second case, wireline operators began competing against wireless operators. If neither of the technologies were popular, they would have had little impact. However, they were popular and thus triggered a cycle of liberalization—for VOIP, massive illegal Internet use; for Little Smart, under-the-counter sales of a cheap and useful service.

This story of challenge, defense, and retrenchment is consistent with the work of Barry Naughton and Yi-Min Lin, who argue that although shifts in ideology or bureaucratic interest may trigger reforms in China, shifts are also sustained by forces generated by society, outside the state realm.[49] In telecommunications, the key social forces are consumers seeking better services and cheaper prices and firms chasing larger market shares. Most notably, the interests of ordinary citizens—when not blocked by bureaucratic interests or ideological constraints—tend to push forward economic reforms. When state-owned operators have flouted MII's rules in an effort to meet market demands, the operators have prevailed. These forces are strong enough of an incentive to undermine the government's efforts to slow down changes in the state-industry framework.

The marked difference between these two cases, however, is which market players in the end appear to have won the lucrative new business opportunity. In the case of VOIP, this service was initiated by small entrepreneurs—*ge ti hu*. In the end, they lost the legal right to offer VOIP. In the cyclical retrenchment, when the ministry legalized the service, licenses were limited to the major state-owned operators. The original VOIP entrepreneurs succeeded in legalizing the service but lacked the political backing to capture the licenses for themselves and for their customers. In the case of Little Smart, the operators who introduced the service were large and politically strong. When asked who in the government backed Little Smart, ultimately allowing it to become successful, one telecommunications executive said, "MII opened one eye, but closed the other." My conversations with mid-level MII officials suggest that the emergence of Little Smart was a serious embarrassment for them. If there was implicit backing of MII for the Little Smart service, then it likely was at the very highest levels. The innovators, wireline operators already well ensconced in the state-industry framework, ended up with the opportunity to profit from their innovation.

In conclusion, although the Chinese state is not able to suppress the rise of new telecommunications services by fiat, it has substantial influence through regulation to channel the benefits to its preferred institutions. Reform-generated market incentives led operators to supply and consumers to demand VOIP and Little Smart, despite government restrictions. These phenomena were substantial enough to threaten MII's established state-industry framework, within which the ministry oversees telecom development. This framework was threatened by new entrepreneurial entrants, in the case of VOIP, and the cross-over of wireline operators into the wireless market, in the case of Little Smart. In the case of VOIP, new entrepreneurs were shut out of the market, and licensed operators within the state-industry framework benefited from the new business. In the case of Little Smart, even today the ministry continues efforts to push wireless and wireline operators to stay within their own prescribed markets, but in the past, the interests of the wireline operators have always prevailed.

9 Does Freeing the Communications Market Require Freeing Communications?

The further China moves away from a command economy, the more its market begins to resemble the markets of other developing countries. Although there might have been a time when explanations of agricultural reform, state enterprise reform, and telecom reform in China would have more in common with each other than each sector would have in common with its counterpart in Brazil or India, today that is increasingly not the case. As the foregoing chapters show, telecom reform in China is best understood in comparison to telecom reform in other countries. This comparison shows how international trends in regulation at key points in time have had a significant impact on the direction of reform in China and will shape the path it takes in the future. When regulatory changes in the Hong Kong market caused the price of calls to the mainland to plummet, Beijing could not ignore the power of freeing the market and moved to introduce more competition. When the Basic Telecommunications Agreement was reached as part of the WTO talks, and one by one countries all over the world separated the regulatory agency from the telecom operator, China joined the trend, even before it joined the WTO. Also, this comparison shows how China deviates from global norms. While countries all over the world are allowing telecom and media operators to enter each others' markets, China officially waits on the sidelines, for ideological reasons preferring to maintain as direct control over the media for as long as possible.

An examination of telecom policy in China contributes to the general study of the Chinese economy. However, that contribution is primarily in the understanding of the trajectory of reform for highly regulated network industries. Chapter 1 alluded to the similarities between the telecommunications service market and other sectors in China, such as banking, airlines, and electricity. Although this study has not plumbed the depths of comparison across sectors, such an investigation would be excellent fodder for future work. For example, the apparent greater openness of the Chinese government to private and foreign participation in these other industries suggests that some similar path may open for telecommunications in the future. The relaxation of retail price controls in telecommunications services suggests that such an approach in other sectors might also be conceivable for the Chinese state.

The direction of telecom reform in China can be explained as the combination of two dynamics, as bureaucratic competition nested in a context of economic and technological change. First, large bureaucracies compete with each other for policy changes that would enhance their own influence, in terms of number of staff, revenue, and political power. This iron fist is a legacy of the command economy, a systemic habit of retaining for the government all the major decisions about the industry. Second, the economic environment in China is constantly changing because the momentum of previous reforms creates opportunities for technical and business innovation, which sharpens competition and increases the need for additional reforms. This reflects the force of the market's invisible hand, which Adam Smith argued works best when society has institutions to establish common defense, to maintain justice, and to provide education for the greater good of society. Maintaining justice in the arena of telecommunications largely means creating the conditions that allow competition while protecting consumers.

Bureaucratic Competition and Its Policy Consequences

Telecom service is an industry with economies of scale, and in China, as in many other countries, there are a small number of large operators. These operators and the government ministries and offices that represent them compete to achieve policy changes favorable to them. Because the Chinese government values consensus, final decisions reflect compromises among these interests. This approach was initially proposed as an explanation for Chinese politics by Lieberthal and Oksenberg in 1988.[1] More recent studies of the Chinese economy are reluctant to place central emphasis on bureaucratic competition. However, much of Lieberthal and Oksenberg's analysis is based on detailed research of the energy and power sector, industries that bear characteristics similar to the telecom sector. It is not surprising, therefore, that this explanation for policy change still remains relevant today. For the telecom sector, in fact, such bureaucratic competition can explain the nature of the telecom policy reform in many countries, not just in China. Consensus building is necessary in these countries, as in China, because in its absence, each constituent interest is powerful enough to undermine any policies set out by the government.

In China's debates on telecom policy reform, there were essentially four main players: MPT, MEI, MRFT, and the State Council. In the early 1990s, when MPT was the sole provider of telecom services, the official waiting list for mainline phones skyrocketed to two million. To alleviate the shortage, the State Council intervened in telecommunications policy and issued regulations allowing other Chinese companies to provide value-added telecommunications services, such as paging.[2] Around this time, MPT had entered into joint ventures with foreign companies to produce telecommunications equipment. In a counterstroke to protect its turf, MEI, the ministry with primary responsibility for the manufacture of electronic equipment, led a coalition of ministries to back a new telecommunications operator—Unicom.[3]

Until they were consolidated in 1998, MEI and MPT were persistent rivals. MPT and Wu Jichuan, its minister during this period, favored the interests of the ministry's old operator—China Telecom. Wu and MPT failed to resolve interconnection disputes with Unicom and resisted the separation of China Telecom into smaller companies. In 1998, when most industry ministries were eliminated in a major administrative reform, Minister Wu survived as head of the new MII, a consolidation of MPT and MEI. Although Wu succeeded in protecting the ministry, the State Council decided to split China Telecom along business lines. Therefore, although he could slow down some changes, he was not powerful enough to counter the State Council efforts at liberalization.

At the time of MII's creation, MRFT also entered the bureaucratic fray. Internet service had been under the authority of MPT, but as the patron ministry of cable television, MFRT was eager to enter. Internet service provided over cable modem technology was booming in other parts of the world. Although MRFT had been demoted to SARFT in the 1998 administrative reform, as the government organization responsible for implementing the Chinese Communist Party Propaganda Department's goals, it retained influence over issues related to communications content and ideology. For example, after the 1998 administrative reform, MII tried to assert regulatory power over broadcasting by stating that new laws would allow broadcasters to provide telecommunications services and vice versa. As of mid-2000, MII officials were announcing that the domestic telecommunications and cable television operators should be able to enter each other's markets to promote competition. However, SARFT counter announcements indicated that they would not accept the opening of the cable television sector to telecommunications companies. SARFT prevailed.

These conflicts among MII, SARFT, and the former MEI enterprises were brokered by the State Council. In the midst of debates on the overall direction of telecommunications policy and occasionally on specific decisions, Premier Zhu Rongji during his tenure lent his clout and reputation to promoting liberalization of the telecommunications sector. When the telecommunications ministry was unable to create a level playing field for competing operators, Premier Zhu, through the State Council, supported several actions to mitigate China Telecom's market power: through separation of China Telecom from the telecommunications ministry in 1998, separation of mobile operations from China Telecom in 1999, and further geographic separation of its northern operations from the rest of China Telecom in 2002. It was the State Council that made decisions on how to organize government authority over telecom, which included gutting the old MPT of operational control over the network. In order to operate the network and run the postal service, MPT previously had hundreds of thousands of employees in offices in every town and city throughout the country. In contrast, the regulatory offices of the ministry that eventually became MII consisted of a few hundred employees with offices only in Beijing and one in every provincial capital. For observers, it appeared that MII remained the patron of telecom operators, occasionally favoring China Telecom more than others, while responsibility for telecom development for overall economic growth lay with the State Council.

Licensing is the policy area most obviously affected by this bureaucratic competition. Firms in China are not free to enter and exit the telecommunications market. The government controls these decisions and only large ministry-backed operators have a chance at getting a license. To date, no other constituency has successfully challenged the State Council's decisions to control entry and exit in the telecommunications market. The State Council maintains a certain state-industry framework that allows rivalry among the admitted but excludes all others that may be interested in participating. As a result of telecom reform, a handful of large, politically well-connected firms have been able to enter the market. The entry of Unicom advanced the interests of MEI, a rival ministry of MPT. The entry of Netcom also advanced the interests of a rival organization, SARFT. Railcom represents the latest—and, as yet, only modestly successful—entry of the Ministry of Railways to compete in telecom.

Divestiture, one of the bluntest tools available to regulators, is another result of bureaucratic competition. China Telecom has been split twice by the government—once to spin off the mobile operator and the second time into northern and southern operators. In each instance, the assets and advantages of the new units were balanced against each other. Making China Mobile independent of China Telecom was intended to give Unicom, a mobile operator, a fairer chance of competition against China Mobile. The second breakup, which joined the advanced Internet network of China Netcom with the less prosperous northern half of China Telecom, was a counterbalance to the prosperous southern half of China Telecom. In 2007, as debates continued to swirl over the possible issuance of licenses for advanced wireless telecommunications services, popularly known as third generation or 3G services, the final decision was again expected to be a brokered compromise among government organizations.

The interconnection drama is another example of fallout from bureaucratic competition. In the early 1990s, when MPT defended China Telecom, China Telecom could refuse interconnection with Unicom, the operator of MEI, with impunity. One reason for the State Council's decision to break up China Telecom was the intractability of the interconnection problem. The solution was to combine MPT and MEI and to split up China Telecom. China Telecom would then be required to treat Unicom the same as it treated its own former mobile arm, now China Mobile. Interconnection improved for China Telecom's competitors, but difficulties were still significant enough to warrant a second break-up of China Telecom in 2002. Although the ministry has established rules, these are consistently circumvented or flouted. Interconnection rules, which govern the terms and conditions of exchanging telecommunications traffic between operators, are the province of MII. However, when disputes arise between operators, the operators themselves often avoid the provincial offices of the MII, who in principle have the authority to mediate, and go directly to the State Council, whose decisions in practice are more effectively binding.

Another area marked by bureaucratic competition is foreign investment. When in the 1990s international telecommunications firms had substantial capital and interest in investing in China, the government relaxed and enforced its foreign investment rules unpredictably. During this period, foreign investors took assurance from the State Council that their investment in Unicom was not illegal. Unicom was especially eager to take in foreign investment because it had fewer sources of capital compared with China Telecom, which was then still backed strongly by the MPT. In the end, it was the State Council that reversed itself on allowing foreign investment in Unicom. This coincided with the first split of China Telecom, designed to put Unicom and China Mobile on more equal footing. Later on, the successful IPO of China Telecom shares on the Hong Kong and New York stock exchanges in 1997 opened new opportunities for foreigners to invest in state-owned firms, but in a manner that minimized their management control. Even with a new set of foreign investment rules stemming from WTO commitments, very few companies have succeeded in investing in telecommunication service operations in China.

Changing Technological and Economic Context

As bureaucratic negotiations proceeded, the context within which they took place continued to evolve. As Naughton and Lin have noted, although shifts in ideology or bureaucratic interest may trigger reforms in China, these shifts are sustained by forces generated by society, outside the state realm.[4] In the main, the outside forces with the most pronounced effect on telecom reform in China are customer demand and technological innovation.

In the late 1990s, the introduction of a technology new to China, the PHS service, blurred the distinction for consumers between wireline and wireless operators. PHS technology allowed the wireline operator China Telecom, and later on also China Netcom, to offer telecom service with a wireless handset at a price much cheaper than cellular service. For years, this Little Smart service was illegal, and therefore, no pricing guidelines existed. Little Smart competed directly against Unicom and China Mobile's cellular service, which is price regulated. Little Smart services, run by the largest state-owned operator, China Telecom, profited at the expense of the mobile operators China Mobile and China Unicom. MII has been powerless to fight China Telecom, now split into China Telecom and China Netcom, in the face of Little Smart's widespread popularity.

Also in the late 1990s, IP technology became easily available, which allowed anyone with an Internet connection to provide international and domestic long distance telephone service at low cost. As with the Little Smart technology, IP telephones' legal status was murky; it was not price regulated yet competed directly against the major operator services, which were price regulated. Different from Little Smart, in its early stages IP telephony threatened the profits of state-owned operators and benefited small entrepreneurs. Consequently, MII banned IP telephony. However, a regulatory experiment demonstrated that state-owned operators could offer IP telephony services profitably. MII then legalized IP telephony for these operators but continued to prohibit small enterprises from entering the market.

Technological innovation challenged mainly two types of regulation: licensing and pricing rules. Licensing rules were undermined as IP telephony enabled small companies to offer service, and Little Smart enabled wireline companies to offer wireless service. The economic incentives for firms to offer these services combined with the economic incentives for consumers to seek them out effectively discredited government efforts to ban both services. In the end, the government reversed its position on both. Technological change also put pressure on the government's pricing policy for telecom services. MII is able to set national pricing guidelines with specific margins for individual operators. However, operators often offer services at lower prices or in alternative packages, often with the knowledge of MII's provincial officials, who are reluctant to act against them. These alternative prices are popular and usually enable some consumers to buy services that they otherwise might not have been able to afford. MII was unable to enforce these rules because the operators had greater incentive to serve the market than to obey the ministry. In the instance of retail prices, MII tried to maintain higher prices than the market would bear in order to protect the government revenue generated by state-owned enterprises, MII officials said. Over time, as the operators continued to lower their prices, the ministry's policy was unsustainable.

Pluralizing Decision Making Can Strengthen the Government's Authority

Currently, as demonstrated by the last three chapters on retail pricing, interconnection, and introduction of new services, the ministry's decisions were all widely ignored and circumvented. In these instances, the iron fist approach toward policymaking inherited from the days of the command economy did not work. The Chinese government faces significant enforcement problems in telecom policy in part because decisions are poorly made. The state's authority is weak because many of its most important decisions are driven by ideology rather than reflecting actual market conditions. Consequently, regulation fails to take into account the enormous incentives for firms and consumers not to comply with the rules—in other words, it is fighting the invisible hand of the market. To improve the situation, regulators in China should base their decisions on information that reflects consideration of all interests involved; they should support the invisible hand rather than work against it. The interest of firms appears to be an expansion of market share. The interest of consumers appears to be either better quality or cheaper service. Consumers react by flocking to discounted rates and new services, whether or not they are legal. In the case of IP telephony and Little Smart, firms' interest and consumer demand for such services override the ministry's desire to protect government revenue. In order to be more effective, the state needs more and better market information. To gain this information may require broadening the scope of views it takes into consideration, in effect pluralizing the government decision-making process.

If the ministry had more fully taken into consideration the interest of firms and consumers, a different regulatory approach with a higher likelihood of compliance possibly could have been adopted. In other countries, regulatory decisions often systematically include procedures for collecting constituent views. For example, in a study of regulatory decision-making processes in Canada, Hong Kong, the United Kingdom, and the United States, there were three main steps to the development or modification of regulations that these markets had in common. First, the regulator developed and publicly distributed the proposed rules. Second, a variety of techniques were used to collect public input on these rules. The most important vehicle in all four markets was the submission of written comments, most of which were also made public. In many instances, firms and individuals had the opportunity to submit additional remarks in response to the first round of comments. Depending on the issues at stake, public hearings or workshops were organized. Finally, when the regulator reached a decision, the basis for the decisions was explained in a written public document, and the basis for rejecting other ideas was also documented. This formal consultation process ensures that new rules are created by the government in full awareness of potential reaction from firms and consumers.[5] Although this is hardly a transition to full democracy, at least greater transparency in government decision making may lead the state to be more effective and may enhance its authority.

A second necessary element to improving policymaking is for the ministry to collect better information on the state of the market. A public consultation would bring out a great deal of market information. However, in China, the question of market data is also closely tied to the reform of state-owned enterprises. On the one hand, the listing of firms on stock exchanges exposes the firms at least to some basic financial accountability, but as of yet, no Chinese telecom operator has exposed all its main operations to such scrutiny. All keep their least profitable operations off the market. In order to make reasoned decisions on interconnection and retail pricing, regulators require detailed cost data, usually reported in financial statements. This is only gradually becoming possible as state-owned enterprises are made more financially account-able to their owner—the state. Cost information, price information, and the direction of market developments are all things regulators usually seek to understand before settling disputes and issuing new rules.

Liberalization of the telecommunications market in the last twenty-five years has led to growth in services and improved the daily lives of millions of Chinese. However, government interests in control-ling information that flows over these networks resulted in limited entry into the market, curtailing competition and preserving substantial state control. Technological change has given firms and consumers the tools to challenge the state's regulatory authority. It is increasingly evident that despite the spectacular growth in telecommunications services over the last two decades and all the benefits that telecommunications service has brought to the lives of people and the development of the economy, some aspects of future telecommunications development may be cur-tailed because the state fails to formulate major policy decisions that reflect actual market conditions. In essence, policy decisions do not take into account the enormous incentives for firms and consumers to subvert the rules. In telecommunications service policy, economic reform and technological change have created an environment where the lack of consultative, pluralistic policymaking weakens the state's authority. Whether the Chinese state, in these circumstances, will accept this lim-ited type of political reform remains to be seen.

While limited political reform would strengthen the state's au-thority, could the economic and technological change that has trans-formed the policymaking context in China also erode the authoritarian control of the government and lead to broader political reform? On the one hand, communications services are booming, subscribership is climbing, and content is expanding. On the other hand, Internet super-vision is strengthening, not weakening, and reports of constraints are growing.[6] Indeed, although the Internet has a longer history and larger presence in the United States than in China, MII's rules governing web-site content already well outstrip those of the United States.[7]

Technological change itself can work in favor of either greater freedom or greater state control. On the one hand, the digitalization of communications services reduces the cost and increases the ease of dis-seminating information, whether via a written text, a video, or some other form. On the other hand, the personalization enabled by the digitalization of communications service—bringing information directly to one's mobile phone or one's personalized e-mail address—means that developing a profile and tracking an individual is much easier as well.

Initial views on the effect of new telecommunications technology were hopeful that the Internet would lessen the authority of the state. In the mid-1990s there were frequent reports that dissidents against the government were successfully using the Internet to communicate. More generally, discussions of the "knowledge economy" suggested that the Internet and other communications technologies had the capacity to open communities that were once previously closed and to change the balance of power between citizens and their governments.[8] Furthermore, both ordinary consumers and state-owned enterprises are readily willing to subvert the rules of the state in order to achieve their own ends. The rapid growth of technologically new services, despite government prohibitions, demonstrates how tenuous the state's regulatory authority is.

From the point of view of consumers, the freedom to choose has dramatically increased as a result of liberalization of the telecommunications market. In telecommunications, the entry of even one new company often significantly changes the range of options for consumers, albeit more modestly than fully opening the market. In China, since the introduction of the second, third, and fourth operator in the market, the number of subscribers has grown very quickly. For consumers, the immediate effect of this partial liberalization of the telecommunications market has meant more services at better prices. As a result of more telecommunications services at better prices, all kinds of new communities have been enabled. As telecommunications liberalization has increased, so has individual freedom. These choices have increased opportunities for individuals to connect with others and to access information. Checking an Internet news list or receiving sports results on a cell phone can create that sense of informed community that bridges time and space.[9] These can be networks of people banding together for political causes or consumers sharing information on the best buys. Within these new communities, information can flow as it never has before.

However, more recent specific studies of China suggest that more caution is necessary in accepting the theory that new communications technology will lead inevitably to political liberalization. Certain ideological factors constrain liberalization in telecommunications in China. The first is that the Chinese government insists on national security grounds that all firms remain Chinese and state-owned, which constrains companies' managerial independence and places key network components under direct state control. Ultimately, this ideological concern is reflected in very limited entry into the market and in efforts to minimize foreign investment. The state's second ideological concern is that because the media have a special role in framing the ideological world of the people, competition in broadcast cannot be allowed as it has been in telecommunications. These principles remain steadfast for the moment, despite evidence that other countries have not needed to retain state ownership to protect national security, in the first instance, and that telecommunications and broadcast are increasingly difficult to separate, in the second.

For decades, the Chinese state has sought to control the flow of information within the country and between China and the outside world. In 1979, Godwin Chu summarized China's four media goals as mobilizing the people, implementing ideological reforms, providing information on Communist Party policies, and reflecting well on those who were ascendant in the Communist Party.[10] Twenty years later, Yuezhi Zhao, in her study of the more commercial media, finds that these four goals remain firmly in place.[11] The cases in this study show that where media and telecom authorities collide, the guardians of ideology usually prevail. Although popular culture flourishes and business information improves, news on politically sensitive subjects still is controlled. In the Chinese media, marketization alone is not creating conditions for independence and free expression. Although it appears that the general liberalizing trend in telecom reform is not reversible, the same cannot be said for services that on depend on the telecom infrastructure for distribution, especially Internet content. Not until the government believes that greater media freedom would serve to strengthen the state, as pluralization of decision making may enhance the government's regulatory authority, is this likely to change.

Notes

Chapter 1

1. Naughton and Yang, *Holding China Together*, 1–23.

2. Yang, *Remaking the Chinese Leviathan*, 291–309.

3. Lieberthal and Oksenberg, *Policy Making in China*, 3–33; Lieberthal and Lampton, *Bureaucracy, Politics, and Decision Making in Post-Mao China*, 1–58.

4. Naughton, *Growing Out of the Plan*, 1–56.

5. Xu, "A Powerhouse of Reform," 123–143.

6. For a more extensive discussion, see Fewsmith, *China Since Tiananmen*.

7. Wang Hu, "Liantong fenchai jianxing jiannan."

8. Zhang and Chen, "Evolution of China's Air Transport Development and Policy Towards International Liberalization," 33.

9. Wong and Wong, "Competition in China's Domestic Banking Industry," 20.

10. Xu and Chen, "The Reform of Electricity Power in the People's Republic of China," 2455.

11. Le, "Reforming China's Airline Industry," 48.

12. Brehem and Macht, "Is a New Broom Sweeping Clean?," 169.

13. Xu and Chen, "The Reform of Electricity Power in the People's Republic of China," 2459.

14. International Telecommunications Union, *World Telecommunication Development Report 2002* (Geneva, 2002), 49.

15. International Telecommunications Union, *Trends in Telecommunications Reform 2004/2005* (Geneva, December 2004), 5.

16. Jordana and Levi-Faur, "Toward a Latin American Regulatory State?," 335–366.

17. Zhu, Zheng, Gao, and Wang, "Environmental Impacts and Benefits of Regional Power Grid Interconnections for China," 1797–1805.

18. Le, "Reforming China's Airline Industry," 54.

19. O'Neill, "Fledgling Airlines Face Uphill Struggle for China Take-Off."

20. Blackman and Wu, "Foreign Direct Investment in China's Power Sector," 702.

21. Hu, "State's Grip Loosens as World Banks on China."

22. Efendioglu, "The Airline Industry in China," 211–221.

23. Xu and Chen, "The Reform of Electricity Power in the People's Republic of China," 2455–2465.

24. See the following news reports: Magnier, "China's Boom Economy Is Starved for Electricity"; and Cohn, "China's Engine Starts to Sputter."

25. See the following news reports: Yao, "Ignored by Banks"; and Bradsher, "China's Informal Lenders Pose Risk to Banks."

Chapter 2

1. Headrick, *The Invisible Weapon*, 7.

2. Baark, *Lightning Wires*, 55.

3. Spence, *The Search for Modern China*, 158–164.

4. *Haifang dang*, Letters dated March 13 and 14, 1865, Document 9, pp. 8–9, as cited in Baark, 73.

5. Baark, 197.

6. Fischer, *American Calling*, 33–54.

7. Wallsten, "Ringing in the Twentieth Century."

8. Thatcher, *The Politics of Telecommunications*, 32–45, 100.

9. Anchordoguy, "Nippon Telegraph and Telephone Company (NTT)," 509–521.

10. He, "A History of Telecommunications in China," 11, 61–62.

11. Post and Telecommunications History Compiling Office, *A History of Contemporary Chinese Postal Service and Telecommunications* (Beijing: People's Post and Telecommunications Publishing House, 1984), as cited in He, "A History of Telecommunications in China," 62.

12. He, "A History of Telecommunications in China," 62–65.

13. Ibid.

14. Xu Yan and Pitt, *Chinese Telecommunications Policy*, 12.

15. He, "A History of Telecommunications in China," 75–79.

16. Ibid., 77–78; She, "Gaobie dianxin juren"; Yeung, "Foreign Firms May Get Little from Bids for China Telecom."

17. See Roller and Waverman, "Telecommunications Infrastructure and Economic Development," 909–923.

Chapter 3

1. Mueller and Tan, *China in the Information Age*, 37–38.

2. Inuk Chung, "Review of the Development and Reform," 11.

3. Interview with business person, conducted by author, March 2003, China.

4. Jardine Fleming Securities, *Asian Telecommunications De-Regulators*, 38; Xu Yan, "The Impact of the Regulatory Framework," 517.

5. Mueller and Tan, *China in the Information Age*, 72.

6. For more discussion, see Stern and Holder, "Regulatory Governance," 33–50; Stern, "What Makes an Independent Regulator Independent?," 67–74; Cowhey and Klimenko, "The WTO Agreement and Telecommunication Policy Reform."

7. For a concise discussion of the history of telecommunications in the United States, Japan, the United Kingdom, and other countries, see Hudson, *Global Connections*.

8. International Telecommunications Union, Development Sector, Study Group 1, "Final Report on Question 8/1."

9. Asia Pacific Economic Cooperation (APEC), "Implementing the WTO Agreement on Basic Telecommunications in APEC Member Economics."

10. Mueller and Tan, *China in the Information Age*, 59–60.

11. Yan, "The Impact of the Regulatory Framework," 517.

12. U.S. Department of State, "Proposed Reorganization of Telecoms Ministry."

13. *Yearbook of China Transportation and Communications 2001*, 236–237.

14. Chetham, "Ministry Reshuffle May Bode Well for Telecoms"; Ella Lee, "Conflicts Should Cloud New Mainland Ministry."

15. U.S. Department of State, "China Telecom."

16. Ella Lee, "Wu Faces Challenge to Unite Ministries."

17. Interview with industry analyst, conducted by author, March 2003, China.

18. Interviews with industry analyst and businessperson, conducted by author, March 2003, China.

19. Yan, "The Impact of the Regulatory Framework," 526–527.

20. Lin Sun, "China Accelerates Reforms."

21. U.S. Department of State, "Proposed Reorganization of Telecoms Ministry."

22. *Beijing Zhongguo Dianzi Bao*, "Information Industry Ministry Outline," 1.

23. Paltridge, "The Development of Broadband Access in OECD Countries."

24. Zhou Qiren, *Shuwang Jingzheng*.

25. Rothman and Barker, "Cable Connections," 20–25.

26. Rothman and Barker, "Cable Connections," 20–25. Figures for 2006 are from http://www.cmmintelligence.com.

27. William Johnson, "Trip Report on Third Sino-International Cable Television Executive Management Conference."

28. Xue, "China's Cable Industry."

29. Interviews with government officials, conducted by author, March 2003, China.

30. Newlands, "Country: The Five-Year Plan."

31. Rothman and Barker, "Cable Connections," 20–25.

32. China Online, "China—MII Pushes Integration of Telecom, Cable Networks."

33. Pepper, Trip report.

34. Rothman and Barker, "Cable Connections," 20–25.

35. Kynge, "China Looks to Ring Changes in Telecoms Sector."

36. Chaffin, Chan, and Ip, "Departments Pull in Different Directions on Media Integration"; Dickie and Yeh, "Viacom Launches Tie-up with a Song and Dance."

37. Kyodo News International, "Breakup of China Telecommunications."

38. Lin Sun, "China Accelerates Reforms."

39. Meeting of author with Chinese and U.S. government officials, Washington DC, March 2002.

40. Tschang, "MII Will Carry Out Commission Plans."

41. Meeting of author with Chinese and U.S. government officials, Washington DC, March 2002.

42. Kynge, "China Looks to Ring Changes in Telecoms Sector."

43. Meeting of author with Chinese and U.S. government officials, Washington DC, March 2002.

44. State-owned Assets Supervision and Administration Commission (SASAC) of the State Council, "Zhongguo guoyou zichan guanli tizhi gaige xin

jieduan" ["China's state-owned assets supervisory system reform enters a new stage"]. News release, May 23, 2003. http://www.sasac.gov.ch.

45. Hu Wang, "Liantong fenchai."

46. Ting Shi, "State Control Spelled out for Strategic Industries," *South China Morning Post*, December 19, 2006.

Chapter 4

1. See Scherer and Ross, *Industrial Market Structure and Economic Performance*, 18–29.

2. See Laffont and Tirole, *Competition in Telecommunications*.

3. Faulhaber, "Public Policy in Telecommunications," 251–282.

4. See Wellenius, "Closing the Gap in Rural Telecommunications"; Wallsten, "An Economic Analysis of Telecom Competition," 1–19.

5. Irvine, "Taiwan Telecoms," 6–7.

6. *Straits Times*, "Business of China's Army Is Also Doing Business."

7. Cary Huang, "Beijing's Decisions Last Week," 11.

8. Pottinger, "China's Military Building Mobile Phone Empire."

9. Cheung, "Hong Kong," 3.

10. *Hong Kong Hsin Pao*, "Enterprises Belonging to Seven Military Regions Must Cut Ties," 2.

11. Unicom, "Annual Report," 9.

12. Mueller and Tan, *China in the Information Age*, 46–49.

13. Katherine Huang, *Elites, Bureaucracy and Policy Learning*, 123–150.

14. *Caijing zazhi bianji bu*, 154.

15. Katherine Huang, *Elites, Bureaucracy and Policy Learning*, 150.

16. *Straits Times*, "Growth of China's Second Phone Carrier Checked by Main Rival."

17. Wang Chuandong, "China United Telecommunications Corp (China Unicom)."

18. FT Asia Intelligence Wire, "China—Government Mulls Spin-off of Telecom Giant"; Bickers, "Phoning Home"; *China Daily*, "China Telecom Break-up Tolls Knell."

19. *Caijing zazhi bianji bu*, 18.

20. Ibid., 17.

21. For a succinct discussion of the circumstances favoring vertical separation or vertical integration, see Gonenc, Maher, and Nicolette, "The Implementation and the Effects of Regulatory Reform."

22. Lin Sun, "China Telecom at Crossroads."

23. *Caijing zazhi bianji bu*, 29.

24. Ibid., 16. Interview with industry analyst, conducted by author, March 2003, China.

25. *Caijing zazhi bianji bu*, 29–31.

26. Fellman and Chan, "Hong Kong Telecom Cuts IDD Charges by About 25%"; Wei and Phan, "Telecoms Price War Heats up in Hong Kong"; Lucas, "Hong Kong Telecom Price War"; Phan and Fellman, "Hong Kong Companies Renew Phone Rate Battle."

27. *Caijing zazhi bianji bu*, 41–43.

28. Xinhua, "Information Ministry to Reorganize China Telecom." Reuters, "Breaking up Is Hard to Do." January 14, 1999.

29. *Hong Kong Ming Pao*, "Zhu Reportedly Breaks Monopoly of Telecom"; *Caijing zazhi bianji bu*, 160–167.

30. Interviews with business person and government official, conducted by author, March 2003, China.

31. Xinhua, "Ministry of Railways Challenges China Telecom's Monopoly."

32. *Caijing zazhi bianji bu*, 141–143.

33. Exchange Telecommunications Newsletters, "Competition Appears Imminent in China."

34. Xinhua, "China's Railways Install Second Tele"; *Caijing zazhi bianji bu*, 142–143.

35. Xinhua, "China's Railways Install Second Tele"; *Caijing zazhi bianji bu*, 142–143.

36. *Caijing zazhi bianji bu*, 143–44.

37. Kynge, "China Backs New Telecoms Operator to Widen Market."

38. Hui and Ng, "China Unicom Puts an End to Union."

39. *Caijing zazhi bianji bu*, 146.

40. Hou, "China Telecom Officially Relinquishes Monopoly"; AFX news, "China Railcom Launches 8080 km Broadband Fibre Network," November 21, 2001.

41. Xinhua, "China Railcom, Satellite Interconnected"; Xiao Hou, "China Telecom, China Railcom Deal Breaks Telecom Monopoly," *China Daily*, June 13, 2001; Xinhua, "PRC Railway Communications Links with China Telecom," September 23, 2001.

42. *Caijing zazhi bianji bu*, 103–106.

43. Ibid., 103–107.

44. Wei, "PRC to Set up Third Government-Backed Telecom Operator."

45. *Caijing zazhi bianji bu*, 108.

46. See China Netcom website: http://www.cnc.net.cn (accessed November 2003).

47. Ingelbrecht, "Ecologist Sows Seed of Change in China."

48. U.S. Department of State, "China: Creating Domestic Competition in Telecom."

49. Kynge, "China Plans to Launch Third State Telecoms Company"; U.S. Department of State, "China: Creating Domestic Competition in Telecom"; *Caijing zazhi bianji bu*, 109–110.

50. *Caijing zazhi bianji bu*,109–110.

51. Ibid., 110.

52. Gharhremani, "China Netcom's Big Connection."

53. Ng, "Merger Proposal Prompts Questions on Sector."

54. Geng Zhicheng, "State Council Approves China Telecom Breakup."

55. Kynge, "China Looks to Ring Changes in Telecoms Sector"; Newlands, "China Telecom Split Yields Fewer Answers"; Geng Zhicheng, "State Council Approves China Telecom Breakup."

56. Kynge, "China Looks to Ring Changes in Telecoms Sector."

57. AFX News, "China Mobile/Unicom Lower on Fears of China Telecom Competition"; Hui Yuk-min, "Rejig Plan Hits Mobile Stocks," *South China Morning Post*, January 10, 2002.

58. Interview with government official, conducted by author, March 2003, China.

59. Interviews with industry analysts, conducted by author, March 2003, China.

60. Interview with government official, conducted by author, March 2003, China; Hui Yuk-min "Telecoms Firms on Notice: Mainland Moves to Boost Competition and Services Through Consolidation into Four Full-Service Giants," *South China Morning Post*, January 9, 2002; Interfax News Agency, "MII Minister: State Council Approves North-South Split of China Telecom," November 30, 2001; Joe Leahy, "Plan to Open Markets Hits Phone Groups," *Financial Times*, January 10, 2002.

61. Ming Juan, "Telecom Witnesses Significant Growth."

62. Ghahremani, "China Netcom's Big Connection."

63. Agence France Presse, "Chinese Government Approves Breakup of Largest Fixed Line Telecom."

64. Ming, "Telecom Witnesses Significant Growth."

65. Interview with businessperson, conducted by author, March 2003, China.

66. Interview with government official, conducted by author, March 2003, China.

67. Interview with industry analyst, conducted by author, March 2003, China.

68. Interview with industry analyst, conducted by author, March 2003, China.

69. Interview with industry analyst, conducted by author, March 2003, China.

70. Wang Hu, "Liantong fenchai"; Xu Ke, "Dianxin: 3G huo fu"; Ming Shuliang, "Sanlou wei xuanbu."

71. See Lieberthal and Lampton, *Bureaucracy, Politics, and Decision Making in Post-Mao China.*

Chapter 5

1. Interview with businessperson, conducted by author, March 2003, China.

2. Baark, *Lightning Wires*, 197.

3. Zhou He, "A History of Telecommunications in China," 11, 61–65.

4. Geng, "China and WTO."

5. Globerman, "Foreign Ownership in Telecommunications," 21–28.

6. Joseph, "Direct Foreign Investment in Telecommunications," 413–426.

7. Georgette Wang, "Foreign Investment Policies, Sovereignty and Growth," 267–282.

8. From China Telecom's website, as quoted in Janda, "Benchmarking a Chinese Offer on Telecommunications," 4, fn5.

9. Zhongguo Tongxun She, "Ban on Foreign Investment in Telecommunications to Remain."

10. Reuters, "China Dims Hopes for Foreign Internet Investment."

11. Agence France Presse, "Three Cities Get Early Lead on JVs."

12. Chan and Ellis, "Life After Unicom?"

13. Chandra, "China-Communications."

14. Hewitt, "China Restricts Role for Foreign Telecoms Firms."

15. Kynge, "China: Telecoms Minister Hangs Up on Foreigners"; Business Wire NewsEdge Corporation, "How China Unicom Treats Agreement with Foreign Partner."

16. Agence France Presse, "China to Keep Telecom Services Closed to Foreigners."

17. Clemetson and Koh, "A Chinese Banquet of Red-Chip Stocks."

18. *China Daily*, "China Telecom (Hong Kong) Has Become the Fourth Largest Company on the Hong Kong Bourse."

19. Wang Yizhao, "Zhongguo Dianxin Weile Gaobie De," 66.

20. Ian Johnson, "China's Venture Ban Could Cost Foreign Firms."

21. Kynge, "China: Telecoms Minister Hangs Up on Foreigners."

22. Meeting between businessperson and author, October 20, 1998, Washington, DC; Cao and Su, "China Unicom Enters Competition Market."

23. Kynge, "China Warns Its Telecoms Partners."

24. Xinhua, "Zhu Rongji on Cutting Telecom Charges," March 15, 1999; Geoffrey Murray, "China Opening Line to Foreign Telecom Share," Kyodo News Service, February 4, 2000.

25. U.S. Department of State, "China Unicom Formally Notifies Partner of Contract Termination."

26. She, "Gaobie dianxin juren"; Chinabiz, "Deals Pave Way for Unicom's US$3b Listing," February 3, 2000.

27. DeWoskin, Kenneth. "The WTO and the Telecommunications Sector in China." *China Quarterly* (2001): 630–654.

28. She, "Gaobie dianxin juren"; Chinabiz, "Deals Pave Way for Unicom's US$3b Listing."

29. Chinabiz, "Unicom Faces Legal Action"; Nuthall, "China OK's Foreign Re-investment in Unicom."

30. Business Wire NewsEdge Corporation, "How China Unicom Treats Agreement with Foreign Partner."

31. China Unicom, Form 20-f, 9.

32. Lam, "Leaders Unhappy with WTO Preparations."

33. Interview with businessperson, conducted by author, March 2003, China.

34. State Council of the People's Republic of China, "The Provisions on the Administration of Foreign-Invested Telecommunications Enterprises."

35. Xinhua, "Minister on Further Opening Telecom Market."

36. China Online, "China-First Telecom Service Joint Venture to Start Operation in February."

37. Wang Yizhao, "Zhongguo Dianxin Weile Gaobie De," 66–68.

38. Donegan, "Feature: China and Japan—Eastern Promise."

39. Interviews with businesspeople, conducted by author, March 2003, China.

40. Naughton, *Growing Out of the Plan*, 1–56.

41. Hui and Wang, "China Telecom Forced to Delay Public Offering."

42. Xinhua, "China Telecom Initial Public Offering Now Fully Subscribed After Relaunch."

43. Yeung, "Foreign Firms May Get Little from Bids for China Telecom."

44. Georgina Lee, "China Netcom Taps Foreign Partners."

45. Yeung, "Foreign Firms May Get Little from Bids for China Telecom."

46. *South China Morning Post*, "State Control a Recipe for Weakness and Sloth."

Chapter 6

1. See Irene Wu, *"Setting up Interconnection Regimes."*

2. Inuk Chung, "Review of the Development and Reform," 61.

3. Xu Yan, "The Impact of the Regulatory Framework," 517; Michael Wang, "China Announces Regulations on Telecommunications Network Interconnection."

4. Inuk Chung, "Review of the Development and Reform," 61.

5. Xu Yan, "The Impact of the Regulatory Framework," 519.

6. Cao and Su, "China Unicom Enters Competition Market."

7. Kynge, "China May Open Up Telecoms."

8. *China Telecom Update*, May 1998.

9. Xinhua, "Unicom Breaks Monopoly in Telephone Service."

10. Kynge, "Telecoms Leader Suffers Monopoly Breach."

11. Cao and Su, "China Unicom Enters Competition Market."

12. Michael Wang, "China Unicom Outlines Development Plans."

13. Michael Wang, "China Announces Regulations on Telecommunications Network Interconnection"; Xu Yan, "The Impact of the Regulatory Framework," 517.

14. Inuk Chung, "Review of the Development and Reform," 61.

15. Michael Wang, "China Announces Regulations on Telecommunications Network Interconnection."

16. Ministry of Information Industry, "Provisional Regulations."

17. China Online, "More Info on China Unicom, China Telecom Deal."

18. Xu Yan, "The Impact of the Regulatory Framework," 526–527.

19. Inuk Chung, "Review of the Development and Reform," 61.

20. Ministry of Information Industry, "Provisional Regulations."

21. Inuk Chung, "Review of the Development and Reform," 62.

22. AFX News, "China Telecom, China Unicom Agree on Interconnection Rules."

23. Interview with businessperson, conducted by author, March 2003, China.

24. Ibid.

25. Interview with government officials, conducted by author, June 2002, China.

26. *China Daily*, "China Railcom Gets Connected."

27. Interview with industry analyst, conducted by author, March 2003, China.

28. Ibid.

29. Interfax News Agency, "China Unicom and China Mobile."

30. Wang Yizhao and Sun Liba, "Xin zifei gaige," 97–102.

31. Ibid.

32. Ibid.

33. Ibid.

34. Interview with government officials, conducted by author, June 2002, China.

35. Ibid.

36. Ibid.

37. Ibid.

38. Interview with government officials, conducted by author, March 2003, China.

39. Ibid.

40. Interview with industry analyst, conducted by author, March 2003, China.

41. Interview with government officials, conducted by author, March 2003, China.

42. Interview with industry analyst, conducted by author, March 2003, China.

43. Ibid.

44. Asia Pacific Economic Cooperation, "APEC Principles of Interconnection."

45. Comisión Internacional de Telecomunicaciones, "CITEL Guidelines and Practices for Interconnection Regulation, 1999."

Chapter 7

1. Wellenius and Stern, *Implementing Reforms in the Telecommunications Sector*, 737.

2. Examples of country-specific examinations of tariff reform include Ros and Banerjee, "Telecommunications Privatization and Tariff Rebalancing"; and Crandall, "Telephone Subsidies, Income Redistribution, and Consumer Welfare." For a general discussion, see Hudson, "Telecommunications Planning for Developing Regions: Extending the Infrastructure," in *Global Connections: International Telecommunications Infrastructure and Policy*, 207–232.

3. Vodafone, *Africa*.

4. Interview with industry analyst, conducted by author, March 2003, China.

5. Interview with government officials, conducted by author, March 2003, China.

6. He, "Dianxin zifei guanzhi tizhi de quefa yu wanshan mubiao," 269–277.

7. Ibid.

8. Ibid.

9. Ure, "China's Telecommunications."

10. Ibid.

11. Xinhua, "MII Plans to Lower Telecom Fees 'Significantly.'"

12. Munish, "China Telecom Slashes Fees."

13. Hong, "Zhongguo Dianxin ye de Fazhan yu Gaige," 111.

14. *Asian Wall Street Journal*, "China Mobile-Phone Fee Cuts."

15. Dow Jones International News, "China Hubei Province Stops Local Cellular Rate Cut."

16. Xinhua, "Government to Monitor Charges on Mobile Telecom Service."

17. *China Daily*, "China to Build IP Network."

18. Feng, "Opinion: Less Is More for Mobile Phones."

19. Xinhua, "China Cuts Mobile Phone Fees."

20. Jin, "Opinion: Customers Need More Protection."

21. Ibid.

22. Wang Hui, "Real Competition Can Help"; China Netcom, "Telecom in China."

23. China Netcom, "Telecom in China."

24. Taili Wang, "Asian Legal Briefing."

25. Interview with government officials, conducted by author, April 2002, China.

26. Zhao Huanxin, "Phone Rates Reduction May Trigger Price War."

27. Interview with government officials, conducted by author, April 2002, China.

28. Qian, "The Rise and Fall of Telecommunications Tariffs."

29. Xinhua, "China Cancels Telephone Installation Charges."

30. Newlands, "Connect Fee Scrap Knocks Chinese Entrants."

31. Asiaport, "Beijing Looses Prices Control on Telecom Cards."

32. Interview with government officials, conducted by author, April 2002, China.

33. Interview with government official, conducted by author, April 2002, China.

34. U.S. Information Technology Office, "China's Telecom Service Prices Soon to Be Determined by the Market."

Chapter 8

An earlier version of this chapter was published as "The Triumphant Consumer? VOIP, 'Little Smart,' and Telecom Service Reform in China," in *Information Technologies and International Development* 3 (Summer 2006): 53–66.

1. Naughton, *Growing Out of the Plan*, 1–56.

2. For a more detailed technical discussion, see Taggart and Kelly, "IP Telephony Workshop."

3. Zhou Qiren, *Shuwang jingzheng*; Peter Lovelock. "IP Telephony and the Internet: China Case Study," International Telecommunications Union's Third World Telecommunications Policy Forum, Geneva, Switzerland, March 7–9, 2001.

4. Michael Wang, "Contradictions on Internet Telephony in China"; Pomfret, "In China, a Telecom Free-for-All."

5. Zhou Qiren, *Shuwang jingzheng*.

6. Kynge, "China: Legal Clash Erupts over Internet."

7. Kynge, "China: Court Rules Internet Telephony Is Legal."

8. Zhou Qiren, *Shuwang jingzheng*.

9. Kynge, "China: Legal Clash Erupts over Internet."

10. Holland, "PRC Declares Internet Phone Service Illegal."

11. Zhou Qiren, *Shuwang jingzheng*.

12. Ibid.

13. Zhao Huanxin, "Ministry Not to Open Internet Phone, Fax Sectors."

14. Michael Wang, "Contradictions on Internet Telephony in China."

15. Wang Chuandong, "Internet Phone Services," 6.

16. Michael Wang, "China Internet Protocol Phone Services."

17. China Online, "Jitong, China's Number Three Telecom Company."

18. Michael Wang, "China Internet Protocol Phone Services."

19. Dong, "New IP Network Kicks Off."

20. Interview with government official, conducted by author, March 14, 2003, China.

21. U.S. Department of State, "ISP's, ICP's, and IP Telephony in China."

22. *South China Morning Post*, "Shanghai Web Expert Jailed," 8.

23. U.S. Department of State, "ISP's, ICP's, and IP Telephony in China."

24. China Online, "China Telecom Accused of Unfair Competition, Again."

25. U.S. Department of State, "VOIP in China."

26. Interview with government officials, conducted by author, March 2003, China.

27. U.S. Department of State, "VOIP in China."

28. "2005 Annual Report and 2006 Interim Report," http://www.tom.com.cn.

29. Hui, "Unicom Expects Regulator to Pull Plug on Rival"; Hui, "Main Fixed-line Firms."

30. *Financial Times*, "Little Smart Launched in Beijing."

31. Xin, *Dianxin qiye zhanlue guanli.*

32. Hui, "Unicom Expects Regulator to Pull Plug on Rival."

33. Hou, "Little Smart Packs a Big Threat."

34. AFX News, "China Netcom to Offer Xiaolingtong Service."

35. Hou, "Growth on Hold for Little Smart Wireless Devices."

36. MFC Insight Update, "A Rush of Blood to the Head."

37. Olivia Chung, "Little Smart Move Upsets Mobile Firms."

38. *China Daily*, "Consumers Should Be the Top Priority."

39. Li Jialu, "Xiao lingtong gei xiaofeizhe tigongle chayi xing xuanze" ["Little Smart provides consumers significant different choice:], Xinhua News Agency, April 10, 2003.

40. Wu Zhong, "Little Smart Threatens Giants"; Financial Times Global Newswire, "Little Smart Expands."

41. Financial Times Global Newswire, "Calls Growing to Better Regulate Little Smart."

42. Wu Zhong, "Telecom Players Gird for Battle."

43. MFC Insight Update, "Carriers Canoodlings."

44. Kan, 2003; Hou, June 21, 2002.

45. Kan, Presentation, Beijing University of Posts and Telecommunications for United States Information Technology Office.

46. Interviews with government officials, conducted by author, March 2003, China.

47. For a discussion of the advanced services that VOIP can provide, see Hussain, "Trends in IP Technology." For more on early regulatory acceptance of VOIP in Europe, Japan, and the United States, see Ono and Aoki, "Convergence and New Regulatory Frameworks," 817–838.

48. For further information, see documentation by the Telecommunications Regulatory Authority of India, such as "Unified Licensing Recommendation," http://www.trai.gov.in/recomodifiedfinal.pdf.

49. Yi-min Lin, "Economic Institutional Change in Post-Mao China," 26–51; Naughton, *Growing Out of the Plan.*

Chapter 9

1. Lieberthal and Oksenberg, *Policy Making in China*, 3–33.

2. Inuk Chung, "Review of the Development and Reform of the Telecommunications Sector in China," 11.

3. Interview with businessperson, conducted by author, March 2003, China.

4. See Yi-min Lin, "Economic Institutional Change in Post-Mao China," 26–51; Naughton. *Growing Out of the Plan.*

5. Irene Wu, "Traits of an Independent Communications Regulator" and "Who Regulates Phones, Television and the Internet?"

6. See Kalathil and Boas, *Open Networks, Closed Regimes*, 13–42; Chase and Mulvenon, *You've Got Dissent!*; Berman, "Testimony Before the U.S.-China Economic and Security Review Commission."

7. Interview with government official conducted by the author, March 2003, China.

8. Examples include the following: Central News Agency—Taiwan, "Internet Being Used to Promote Freedom of Expression in China"; and Tang, "China Goes Cyber."

9. For a view on how newspapers and television enable public spheres, see Anderson, *Imagined Communities*; and Thompson, *Media and Modernity.*

10. Chu, *Moving a Mountain*, 57–75.

11. Yuezhi Zhao, *Media, Market, and Democracy in China*, 47–51.

Bibliography

Chinese names are alphabetized by full name with the family name preceding the given name.

AFX News. "China Mobile/Unicom Lower on Fears of China Telecom Competition." December 20, 2001.

———. "China Netcom Starts Building Wireless Network in Rural Beijing." February 18, 2003.

———. "China Netcom to Offer Xiaolingtong Service in Beijing Soon." June 21, 2002.

———. "China Railcom Launches 8080 km Broadband Fibre Network." November 21, 2001.

———. "China Telecom, China Unicom Agree on Interconnection Rules." October 9, 2001.

Agence France Presse. "China to Keep Telecom Services Closed to Foreigners." August 26, 1997.

———. "Chinese Government Approves Breakup of Largest Fixed Line Telecom." December 11, 2001.

———. "Three Cities Get Early Lead on JVs." January 6, 2000.

Anchordoguy, Marie. "Nippon Telegraph and Telephone Company (NTT) and the Building of a Telecommunications Industry in Japan." *Business History Review* 75 (Autumn 2001): 509–521.

Anderson, Benedict. *Imagined Communities: Reflections on the Origin and Spread of Nationalism.* London: Verso, 1983.

Asia Pacific Economic Cooperation (APEC). "APEC Principles of Interconnection." May 14, 1999. http://www.apectelwg.org/apecdata/telwg/int+A32erTG/principl.html.

———. "Implementing the WTO Agreement on Basic Telecommunications in APEC Member Economics—Questionnaires Project (TEL 02/99T)." March 2000. Exhibit 2.1. http://www.apectelwg.org.

Asian Wall Street Journal. "China Mobile-Phone Fee Cuts." May 28, 1999.

Asiaport. "Beijing Looses Prices Control on Telecom Cards." February 6, 2002.

Baark, Erik. *Lightning Wires: The Telegraph and China's Technological Modernization, 1860–1890.* Westport, CT: Greenwood Press, 1997.

Beijing Zhongguo Dianzi Bao. "Information Industry Ministry Outline." July 10, 1998. Translated by Foreign Broadcast Information Service.

Berman, Kenneth, "Testimony Before the U.S.-China Economic and Security Review Commission: China's State Control Mechanisms and Methods." Broadcasting Board of Governors, April 14, 2005. http://www.uscc.gov/hearings/2005hearings/written_testimonies/05_04_14wrts/berman_kenneth_wrts.htm.

Bickers, Charles. "Phoning Home: Telecoms Restructuring in China Aids Local Firms." *Far Eastern Economic Review,* February 18, 1999.

Blackman, Allen, and Xun Wu. "Foreign Direct Investment in China's Power Sector: Trends, Benefits and Barriers." *Energy Policy* 27 (1999): 695–711.

Bradsher, Keith. "China's Informal Lenders Pose Risk to Banks." *New York Times,* November 9, 2004.

Brehem, Stefan, and Christian Macht. "Is a New Broom Sweeping Clean? The Emergence of the China Banking Regulatory Commission." *Aussenwirtschaft,* June 2005, 169–207.

Business Wire NewsEdge Corporation. "How China Unicom Treats Agreement with Foreign Partner." June 20, 2000.

Caijing zazhi bianji bu. *Guanzhi de huanghun: Zhongguo dianxin ye wanyi yuan chongzu shilu* [The dusk of control: The true story of China's telecommunications industry trillion yuan reorganization]. Beijing: Social Sciences Documentation Publishing House, 2003.

Cao Jian and Su Jianchan. "China Unicom Enters Competition Market." Xinhua News Service, September 6, 1998.

Central News Agency—Taiwan. "Internet Being Used to Promote Freedom of Expression in China." October 2, 1999.

Chaffin, Joshua, Jeanette Chan, and Bianca Ip. "Departments Pull in Different Directions on Media Integration." *Financial Times,* May 23, 2007.

Chan, Jeanette, and Marcia Ellis. "Life After Unicom? All May Not Be Lost for Alternative Telecom Investment Structures." *Project Finance Models for Greater China*. Hong Kong: Asia Law and Practice, 1999.

Chandra, Rajiv. "China-Communications: Dial 'S' for Secrecy." Inter Press Service, November 28, 1994.

Chase, Michael, and James Mulvenon. *You've Got Dissent! Chinese Dissident Use of the Internet and Beijing's Counter-Strategies*. Washington, DC: RAND, 2002.

Chen Zhiming. "Information Ministry Says Telecom Rate Adjustments Expected Soon." *China Daily*, November 5, 2000.

Chetham, Andrew. "Ministry Reshuffle May Bode Well for Telecoms." *South China Morning Post*, February 28, 1998.

China Daily. "China Railcom Gets Connected." January 31, 2002.

———. "China Telecom Break-up Tolls Knell for Remaining Monopoly Sectors." February 8, 1999.

———. "China Telecom (Hong Kong) Has Become the Fourth Largest Company on the Hong Kong Bourse." December 2, 1997.

———. "China to Build IP Network." April 30, 1999.

———. "Consumers Should Be the Top Priority." March 12, 2003.

China Netcom. "Telecom in China: Regulatory Environment." www.cnc.net.cn (accessed November 2003).

China Online. "China-First Telecom Service Joint Venture to Start Operation in February." December 19, 2001.

———. "China—MII Pushes Integration of Telecom, Cable Networks." December 18, 2001.

———. "China Telecom Accused of Unfair Competition, Again." April 28, 2000.

———. "Jitong, China's Number Three Telecom Company, Hits Big with New IP." May 28, 1999.

———. "More Info on China Unicom, China Telecom Deal." January 19, 2000.

China Unicom. Form 20-f. Filed with the U.S. Securities and Exchange Commission, Washington, DC. Commission file number 1-15028.

Chinabiz. "Deals Pave Way for Unicom's US$3b Listing." February 3, 2000.

———. "Unicom Faces Legal Action." June 8, 2000.

Chu, Godwin. *Moving a Mountain: Cultural Change in China*. Honolulu: University Press of Hawaii, 1979.

Chung, Inuk. "Review of the Development and Reform of the Telecommunications Sector in China." Paris: Organisation of Economic Co-operation and Development, March 13, 2003.

Chung, Olivia. "Little Smart Move Upsets Mobile Firms." *Financial Times Global Newswire*, February 25, 2003.

Clemetson, Lynette, and Barbara Koh. "A Chinese Banquet of Red-Chip Stocks." *Newsweek*, October 27, 1997.

Cohn, Martin Regg. "China's Engine Starts to Sputter." *Toronto Star*, August 8, 2004.

Comisión Internacional de Telecomunicaciones. "CITEL Guidelines and Practices for Interconnection Regulation, 1999." http://www.citel.oas.org/pcc1/ guidelines /guidelines%20and %20practices.doc.

Cowhey, Peter, and Mikhail Klimenko. "The WTO Agreement and Telecommunication Policy Reform." Washington, DC: World Bank Policy Research Working Paper No. WPS2601, May 31, 2001.

Crandall, Robert. "Telephone Subsidies, Income Redistribution, and Consumer Welfare." In *Implementing Reforms in the Telecommunications Sector: Lessons from Experience*, edited by Bjorn Wellenius and Peter Stern, pp. 400–420. Washington, DC: World Bank, 1994.

DeWoskin, Kenneth. "The WTO and the Telecommunications Sector in China." *China Quarterly* (2001): 630–654.

Dickie, Muriel, and Andrew Yeh. "Viacom Launches Tie-up with a Song and Dance." *Financial Times*, October 19, 2006.

Donegan, Michelle. "Feature: China and Japan—Eastern Promise." *Communications Week International*, February 4, 2002.

Dong Xue. "New IP Network Kicks Off, Covering 12 Cities." *China Daily*, June 20, 1999.

Dow Jones International News. "China Hubei Province Stops Local Cellular Rate Cut." May 26, 1999.

Efendioglu, Alev. "The Airline Industry in China: Evolution and Competitive Dynamics." In *Chinese Economic Transition and International Marketing Strategy*, edited by Ilan Alon, pp. 211–221. Westport, CT: Praeger, 2003.

Exchange Telecommunications Newsletters. "Competition Appears Imminent in China." July 23, 1999.

Faulhaber, Gerald. "Public Policy in Telecommunications: The Third Revolution." *Information Economics and Policy* 7 (1995): 251–282.

Fellman, Joshua, and Biddy Chan. "Hong Kong Telecom Cuts IDD Charges by About 25%." Bloomberg News Service, January 4, 1999.

Feng, Qihua. "Opinion: Less Is More for Mobile Phones." *China Daily*, December 26, 2000.

Fewsmith, Joseph. *China Since Tiananmen: Politics of Transition*. Cambridge: Cambridge University Press, 2001.

Financial Times. "New Users of China's Little Smart Reaches 10 million." January 14, 2003.

Financial Times Global Newswire. "Calls Growing to Better Regulate Little Smart." August 7, 2002.

————. "Little Smart Expands." March 12, 2003.

————. "Little Smart Launched in Beijing." March 13, 2003.

Fischer, Claude S. *American Calling: A Social History of the Telephone to 1940*. Berkeley: University of California Press, 1992.

FT Asia Intelligence Wire. "China—Government Mulls Spin-off of Telecom Giant into Independent Entities." January 12, 1999.

Geng Zhicheng. "China and WTO." *Hong Kong Ta Kung Pao*, November 25, 1999.

Gesteland, Lester. "State Council Approves China Telecom Breakup, Sector Consolidation." China Online, December 17, 2001.

Ghahremani, Yasmin. "China Netcom's Big Connection," *Asiaweek*, November 2, 2001.

Globerman, Steven. "Foreign Ownership in Telecommunications: A Policy Perspective." *Telecommunications Policy* 19 no. 10 (1995): 21–28.

Gonenc, Raul, Maria Maher, and Giuseppe Nicolette. "The Implementation and the Effects of Regulatory Reform: Past Experience and Current Issues." Paris: Organisation of Economic Cooperation and Development (OECD) Economic Studies, No. 32, 2000.

He Xia. "Dianxin zifei guanzhi tizhi de quefa yu wanshan mubiao." In *Zhongguo Jichu Sheshi Chanye de Guizhi Gaige yu Fazhan*, edited by Zhang Xinzhu, pp. 269–277. Beijing: Guojia Xingzheng Xue Yuan, 2002.

He Zhou. "A History of Telecommunications in China: Development and Policy Implications." In *Telecommunications and Development in China*, edited by Paul S. N. Lee, pp. 55–88. Cresskill, NJ: Hampton Press, 1997.

Headrick, Daniel R. *The Invisible Weapon: Telecommunications and International Politics, 1851–1945*. New York: Oxford University, 1991.

Hewitt, Giles. "China Restricts Role for Foreign Telecoms Firms." Agence France Presse, April 11, 1995.

Holland, Lorien. "PRC Declares Internet Phone Service Illegal." Agence France Presse, February 4, 1999.

Hong Kong Hsin Pao. "Enterprises Belonging to Seven Military Regions Must Cut Ties with the Military Within Three Years, Analysts Say Prospects for Some Hong Kong Companies Should Be Reassessed." July 24, 1998, p. 2.

Hong Kong Ming Pao. "Zhu Reportedly Breaks Monopoly of Telecom." April 30, 1999, p. A24.

Hong Xiangdong. "Zhongguo Dianxin ye de Fazhan yu Gaige." In *Zhongguo Jichu Sheshi Chanye de Guizhi Gaige yu Fazhan,* edited by Zhang Xinzhu, pp. 110–133. Beijing: Guojia Xingzheng Xue Yuan, 2002.

Hou Mingjuan. "China Telecom Officially Relinquishes Monopoly of Fixed-Line Phone Market." *China Daily,* July 7, 2001.

———. "Growth on Hold for Little Smart Wireless Devices." Financial Times Global Newswire, July 29, 2002.

———. "Little Smart Packs a Big Threat." Financial Times Global Newswire, June 21, 2002.

Hu, Bei. "State's Grip Loosens as World Banks on China: Foreign Investments, Multibillion-Dollar Listings and Government Bailouts Mark a Period of Seismic Restructuring Among Mainland Lenders." *South China Morning Post,* October 1, 2005.

Hu, Wang. "Liantong fenchai: Jian xing jian nan" ["Unicom break-up: By degrees easier, by degrees harder"]. *Caijing,* January 8, 2007.

Huang, Cary, "Beijing's Decisions Last Week to Order the Military to Give up Its Business Empire and Turn over a Military-Run Brokerage Are Welcome Moves." *Hong Kong Standard,* July 28, 1998, 11.

Huang, Katherine. *Elites, Bureaucracy and Policy Learning; a Case Study of Facilities-Based Competition Policymaking in China's Telecommunications Restructuring.* PhD diss., George Washington University, 2001.

Hudson, Heather. *Global Connections: International Telecommunications Infrastructure and Policy.* New York: Van Nostrand Reinhold, 1997.

Hui Yuk-min. "Main Fixed-line Firms Set to Enjoy Growth Before 3G." *South China Morning Post,* March 3, 2003.

———. "Rejig Plan Hits Mobile Stocks." *South China Morning Post,* January 10, 2002.

———. "Telecoms Firms on Notice: Mainland Moves to Boost Competition and Services Through Consolidation into Four Full-Service Giants." *South China Morning Post,* January 9, 2002.

———. "Unicom Expects Regulator to Pull Plug on Rival; Cheaper Alternative Faces Loss of Spectrum." *South China Morning Post,* September 24, 2001.

———, and Eric Ng. "China Unicom Puts an End to Union; Lack of Present Synergy Cited as Mainland's No. 2 Leaves Door Open." *South China Morning Post,* October 3, 2001.

———, and Wang Xiangwei. "China Telecom Forced to Delay Public Offering: Relaunch Next Week After Poor International Demand." *South China Morning Post,* November 1, 2002.

Hussain, Farooq. "Trends in IP Technology: Their Impact on the Traditional Telephony Carrier World." Paris: Organisation of Economic Co-operation and Development. Working Party on Telecommunication and Information Services Policies, March 20, 2002.

Ingelbrecht, Nick. "Ecologist Sows Seed of Change in China." *Communications Week International*, July 19, 1999.

Interfax News Agency. "China Unicom and China Mobile Reach Network Interconnection and Account Settlement Agreement." November 16, 2001.

———. "MII Minister: State Council Approves North-South Split of China Telecom." November 30, 2001.

International Telecommunications Union (ITU), Development Sector, Study Group 1. "Final Report on Question 8/1." Document 1/204(Rev.1)—E. November 7, 2001. http://www.itu.int/ITU-D/study_groups/SGP_1998 -2002/SG1.

———. "ITU World Indicators 2003." Win*STARS 4.2. Geneva. http://www. itu.int (accessed May 2003).

———. Trends in Telecommunications Reform 2004/2005. Geneva, December 2004.

Irvine, Craig. "Taiwan Telecoms." Hong Kong: Merrill Lynch, October 12, 1999.

Janda, Richard. "Benchmarking a Chinese Offer on Telecommunications: Context and Comparison." *International Journal of Communications Law and Policy*, no. 2 (Winter 1998/99): 1–28.

Jardine Fleming Securities. *Asian Telecommunications De-Regulators*. Hong Kong: Fourth quarter, 1996.

Jin Zeqing. "Opinion: Customers Need More Protection." *China Daily*, August 14, 2000.

Johnson, Ian. "China Dashes Deregulation Hopes as It Puts off Telecom Breakup." *Wall Street Journal*, December 2, 1998.

———. "China's Venture Ban Could Cost Foreign Firms." *Wall Street Journal*, September 23, 1998.

Johnson, William. Federal Communications Commission. "Trip Report on Third Sino-International Cable Television Executive Management Conference." Beijing, March 26, 2002.

Jordana, Jacint, and David Levi-Faur. "Toward a Latin American Regulatory State? The Diffusion of Autonomous Regulatory Agencies Across Countries and Sectors." *International Journal of Public Administration* 29(4–6): 335–66.

Joseph, Richard. "Direct Foreign Investment in Telecommunications: A Review of Attitudes in Australia, New Zealand, France, Germany, and the UK." *Telecommunications Policy* 19(5): 413–426.

Kalathil, Shanthi, and Taylor C. Boas. *Open Networks, Closed Regimes: The Impact of the Internet on Authoritarian Rule.* Washington, DC: Carnegie Endowment for International Peace, 2003.

Kan Kaili. Presentation by Professor, Beijing University of Posts and Telecommunications, U.S. Information Technology Office (USITO). March 10, 2003.

Kynge, James. "China Backs New Telecoms Operator to Widen Market." *Financial Times*, December 4, 2000.

———. "China: Court Rules Internet Telephony Is Legal." *Financial Times Online*, January 22, 1999.

———. "China: Legal Clash Erupts over Internet." *Financial Times Online*, January 26, 1999.

———. "China Looks to Ring Changes in Telecoms Sector." *Financial Times*, October 17, 2001.

———. "China May Open Up Telecoms." *Financial Times*, June 3, 1998.

———. "China Plans to Launch Third State Telecoms Company." *Financial Times*, October 27, 1999.

———. "China: Telecoms Minister Hangs Up on Foreigners." *Financial Times*, November 5, 1998.

———. "China Warns Its Telecoms Partners." *Financial Times*, October 30, 1998.

———. "Telecoms Leader Suffers Monopoly Breach." *Financial Times*, July 20, 1998.

Kyodo News International. "Breakup of China Telecommunications Offers Hope for Competition." February 12, 1999.

Laffont, Jean-Jacques, and Jean Tirole. *Competition in Telecommunications.* Cambridge: MIT Press, 2000.

Lam, Willy Wo-Lap. "Leaders Unhappy with WTO Preparations." *South China Morning Post*, June 23, 2000.

Lampton, David. "A Plum for a Peach: Bargaining, Interest, and Bureaucratic Politics in China." In *Bureaucracy, Politics, and Decision Making in Post-Mao China*, edited by Kenneth Lieberthal and David Lampton, pp. 33–58. Berkeley: University of California Press, 1992.

Lan Xue. "China's Cable Industry: Too Much Smoke in the Air." Hong Kong: Merrill Lynch, April 12, 2000.

Le, Thuong T. "Reforming China's Airline Industry: From State Owned Monopoly to Market Dynamics." *Transportation Journal* (Winter 1997): 45–62.

Leahy, Joe. "Plan to Open Markets Hits Phone Groups." *Financial Times*, January 10, 2002.

Lee, Ella. "Conflicts Should Cloud New Mainland Ministry." *South China Morning Post*, March 17, 1998.

———. "Wu Faces Challenge to Unite Ministries." *South China Morning Post*, March 24, 1998.

Lee, Georgina. "China Netcom Taps Foreign Partners." *South China Morning Post*, March 23, 2006.

Lee, Paul S. N., ed. *Telecommunications and Development in China*. Cresskill, NJ: Hampton Press, 1997.

Li Jialu. "Xiao lingtong gei xiaofeizhe tigongle chayi xing xuanze" ["Little Smart provides consumers significant different choice"], Xinhua News Agency, April 10, 2003.

Lieberthal, Kenneth, and David Lampton. *Bureaucracy, Politics, and Decision Making in Post-Mao China*. Berkeley: University of California, 1992.

Lieberthal, Kenneth, and Michel Oksenberg. *Policy Making in China: Leaders, Structures, and Processes*. Princeton, NJ: Princeton, 1988.

Lin Sun. "China Accelerates Reforms." FT Asia Intelligence Wire, April 1, 1999.

———. "China Telecom at Crossroads, New Uncertainties." FT Asia Intelligence Wire, January 1, 1999.

Lin, Yi-min. "Economic Institutional Change in Post-Mao China." *The Chinese Economy* 35 (3): 26–51.

Lovelock, Peter. "IP Telephony and the Internet: China Case Study." International Telecommunications Union's Third World Telecommunications Policy Forum, Geneva, Switzerland, March 7–9, 2001. http://www.itu.int.

Lucas, Louise. "Hong Kong Telecom Price War." Bloomberg News Service, January 5, 1999.

Magnier, Mark. "China's Boom Economy Is Starved for Electricity." *Los Angeles Times*, September 4, 2004.

MFC Insight Update. "Carriers Canoodlings." April 21, 2003.

———. "A Rush of Blood to the Head." February 26, 2003.

Ming Juan. "Telecom Witnesses Significant Growth." *China Daily*, January 15, 2002.

Ming Shuliang, "Sanbu wei xuanbu dianxin chongzu hou dong" ["Behind the three ministries' telecom restructuring announcement"], *Caijing*, May 25, 2008.

Ministry of Information Industry. "Provisional Regulations for Management of Interconnection Between Telecommunications Networks," November 1999.

———. "Guonei changtu dianhua zifei tiaozheng biao" ["Schedule of adjusted domestic long distance telecommunications tariffs"] and "Guoji ji gang au tai dianxinye yewu zifei" ["Tariffs for international, Hong Kong, Macau, Taiwan telecommunications service"], March 2003. http://www.mii.gov.cn/mii/hyze/zfsy.html.

Mueller, Milton, and Zixiang Tan. *China in the Information Age: Telecommunications and the Dilemmas of Reform*. Washington, DC: Center for Strategic and International Studies, 1997.

Munish, Mukil. "China Telecom Slashes Fees." *Hong Kong Standard*, December 23, 1998.

Murray, Geoffrey. "China Opening Line to Foreign Telecom Share." Kyodo News Service, February 4, 2000.

Naughton, Barry. *Growing Out of the Plan: Economic Reform in China*. Cambridge: Cambridge University Press, 1995.

———, and Dali Yang. *Holding China Together: Diversity and National Integration in the Post-Deng Era*. Cambridge: Cambridge University Press, 2004.

Newlands, Mike. "China Telecom Split Yields Fewer Answers." *Communications Week International*, December 17, 2001.

———. "Connect Fee Scrap Knocks Chinese Entrants." *Communications Week International*, July 16, 2001.

———. "Country: The Five-Year Plan." *Communications International Online*, September 1, 2001.

Ng, Eric. "Merger Proposal Prompts Questions on Sector." *South China Morning Post*, October 1, 2001.

Nuthall, Keith. "China OK's Foreign Re-investment in Unicom." *Total Telecom*, May 25, 2000.

O'Neill, Mark. "Fledgling Airlines Face Uphill Struggle for China Take-off." *South China Morning Post*, March 17, 2005.

Ono, R., and K. Aoki. "Convergence and New Regulatory Frameworks: A Comparative Study of Regulatory Approaches to Internet Telephony." *Telecommunications Policy* 22, no. 10 (1998): 817–838.

Paltridge, Sam. "The Development of Broadband Access in OECD Countries." Paris: Organisation of Economic Co-operation and Development, October 29, 2001. http://www.oecd.org/dataoecd/48/33/2475737.pdf.

Pepper, Robert, Federal Communications Commission Trip report. April 1, 2000.

Phan, Anh-Thu, and Joshua Fellman. "Hong Kong Companies Renew Phone Rate Battle." Bloomberg News Service, January 15, 1999.

Pomfret, John. "In China, a Telecom Free-for-All." *Washington Post*, January 25, 1999.

Pottinger, Matt. "China's Military Building Mobile Phone Empire." Reuters, February 15, 2000.

Qian Puqun. "The Rise and Fall of Telecommunications Tariffs Should Be Viewed Objectively." *Guangming Ribao*. As posted without date on http://www.mii.gov.cn (accessed April 2003).

Reuters. "Breaking Up Is Hard to Do." January 14, 1999.

———. "China Dims Hopes for Foreign Internet Investment." December 13, 1999.

Roller, Lars-Hendrik, and Leonard Waverman. "Telecommunications Infrastructure and Economic Development: A Simultaneous Approach." *American Economic Review*, September 2001, 909–923.

Ros, Agustin, and Aniruddha Banerjee. "Telecommunications Privatization and Tariff Rebalancing: Evidence from Latin America." Working Paper, National Economic Research Association. Cambridge, MA, May 2000.

Rothman, Warren, and Jonathan Barker. "Cable Connections." *China Business Review* (May–June 1999): 20–25.

Scherer, F. M., and David Ross. *Industrial Market Structure and Economic Performance*. Boston: Houghton Mifflin, 1990.

She Yuqing. "Gaobie dianxin juren." *Caijing,* January 2000.

South China Morning Post. "Shanghai Web Expert Jailed for Masterminding Internet Phone Scam." March 7, 2002, p. 8.

———. "State Control a Recipe for Weakness and Sloth." December 19, 2006.

Spence, Jonathan D. *The Search for Modern China.* New York: Norton, 1990.

State Council of the People's Republic of China. "The Provisions on the Administration of Foreign-Invested Telecommunications Enterprises." Decree No. 333. Informal translation, Paul, Wise, and Reilly.

Stern, Jon, "What Makes an Independent Regulator Independent?" *Business Strategy Review*, London (Summer 1997): 67–74.

———, and Stuart Holder. "Regulatory Governance: Criteria for Assessing the Performance of Regulatory Systems, an Application to Infrastructure Industries in the Developing Countries of Asia." *Utilities Policy* 8 (1999): 33–50.

Straits Times. "Business of China's Army Is Also Doing Business." December 9, 1997.

———. "Growth of China's Second Phone Carrier Checked by Main Rival." July 24, 1996.

Ta Ming Cheung. "Hong Kong: Analyst Views Military-Industrial Sector." *South China Morning Post*, July 26, 1998, p. 3.

Taggart, Chris, and Tim Kelly. "IP Telephony Workshop: Background Issues Paper." International Telecommunications Union, Document IPTEL/03, June 14–16, 2000.

Tang, Didi. "China Goes Cyber: Internet Opens Window to Dissent as Leaders Reach for Economic Gain." *Washington Times*, September 25, 2000.

Teo Chian Wei and Anh-Thu Phan. "Telecoms Price War Heats Up in Hong Kong." Bloomberg News Service, January 5, 1999.

Thatcher, Mark. *The Politics of Telecommunications: National Institutions, Convergence, and Change in Britain and France.* Oxford: Oxford University Press, 1999.

Thompson, John. *Media and Modernity: A Social Theory of the Media.* Stanford, CA: Stanford University Press, 1995.

Thurston, Anne. *Muddling Toward Democracy: Political Change in Grassroots China.* Washington, DC: United States Institute of Peace, 1998.

Ting Shi. "State Control Spelled Out for Strategic Industries." *South China Morning Post*, December 19, 2006.

Tschang, Chi-Chu. "MII Will Carry Out Commission Plans." *South China Morning Post*, September 22, 2001.

Unicom. Annual Report 2001, Form 20-F, U.S. Securities and Exchange Commission.

Ure, John. "China's Telecommunications: The Price of Reform." Paper delivered at the China Telecoms Conference, Hong Kong, March 10–11, 1994.

U.S. Department of State. "China: Creating Domestic Competition in Telecom." May 24, 1999.

———. "China Telecom: New Ministry of Information Industries." Beijing, April 15, 1998.

———. "China Unicom Formally Notifies Partner of Contract Termination." Beijing, August 6, 1999.

———. "ISP's, ICP's, and IP Telephony in China." October 19, 1999.

———. "Proposed Reorganization of Telecoms Ministry." Beijing, February 24, 1998.

———. "VOIP in China—Not Until China's Telecom Companies Are Ready." June 20, 2006.

U.S. Information Technology Office. "China's Telecom Service Prices Soon to Be Determined by the Market." March 14, 2002.

U.S. Securities and Exchange Commission. Form 20-F for China Netcom Group Corporation (Hong Kong) Limited for fiscal year ended December 31, 2005. www.sec.gov.

Vodafone. *Africa: The Impact of Mobile Phones*. Vodafone Policy Paper Series, no. 2, March 2005. http://www.vodafone.com/assets/files/en/AIMP _09032005.pdf.

Wallsten, Scott. "An Economic Analysis of Telecom Competition, Privatization and Regulation in Africa and Latin America." *Journal of Industrial Economics* 49, no. 1 (2001): 1–19.

———. "Ringing in the Twentieth Century." World Bank Policy Research Working Paper 2690, October 2001.

Wang Chuandong. "China United Telecommunications Corp (China Unicom), a Fledgling Rival to China Telecom Is Likely to Benefit Greatly from the Current Ministerial Restructuring." *China Daily*, April 1, 1998.

———. "Internet Phone Services." *China Daily* (Business Weekly Supplement, Hong Kong ed.), March 13, 1999, p. 6.

Wang, Georgette. "Foreign Investment Policies, Sovereignty and Growth," *Telecommunications Policy* 27 (2003): 267–282.

Wang Hui. "Real Competition Can Help." *China Daily*, December 18, 2000.

Wang, Michael. "China Announces Regulations on Telecommunications Network Interconnection." Beijing: U.S. Commercial Service, November 15, 1999.

———. "China Internet Protocol Phone Services: Trial Operation to Start." Beijing: U.S. Commercial Service, May 27, 1999.

———. "China Unicom Outlines Development Plans." Beijing: U.S. Commercial Service, April 28, 1999.

———. "Contradictions on Internet Telephony in China." Beijing: U.S. Commercial Service, January 25, 1999.

Wang Rong. "Telecom Services Coming Up Trumps in Guangdong." *China Daily Online*, May 22, 2001.

Wang, Taili. "Asian Legal Briefing: Country File-China: Telecommunications Sector Reform." Briefing by Coudert Brothers, March 2001. http://www. coudert.com/practice/asialegalbrf.htm.

Wang Yizhao. "Zhongguo Dianxin Weile Gaobie De." *Caijing*, September 5, 2003, pp. 66–68.

———, and Sun Liba. "Xin zifei gaige." *Caijing*, February 20, 2003, pp. 97–102.

Wei Ke. "PRC to Set Up Third Government-Backed Telecom Operator." *China Daily*, September 19, 1999.

Wellenius, Bjorn. "Closing the Gap in Rural Telecommunications: Chile 1995–2002." Washington, DC: World Bank Discussion Paper No. 430, February 2002.

———, and Peter Stern. *Implementing Reforms in the Telecommunications Sector: Lessons from Experience*. Washington, DC: World Bank, 1994.

Wong, Richard Y. C., and M. L. Sonia Wong. "Competition in China's Domestic Banking Industry." *Cato Journal* (Spring 2001): 19–41.

Wu, Irene. "Traits of an Independent Communications Regulator: A Search for Indicators." International Bureau Working Paper Series, No. 1, June 2004, U.S. Federal Communications Commission. http://www.fcc.gov/ib.

———. U.S. Federal Communications Commission. "Setting Up Interconnection Regimes: References for Regulators." November 2002. http://www.fcc .gov/globaloutreach.

———. "Who Regulates Phones, Television and the Internet? What Makes a Communications Regulator Independent and Why It Matters." *Perspectives in Politics*, Forthcoming.

Wu Zhong. "Little Smart Threatens Giants." Financial Times Global Newswire, March 11, 2003.

———. "Telecom Players Gird for Battle in Little Smart Wars." *Financial Times*, March 20, 2003.

Xiao Hou. "China Telecom, China Railcom Deal Breaks Telecom Monopoly." *China Daily*, June 13, 2001.

Xin Zhanghong. *Dianxin qiye zhanlue guanli*. Beijing: Beijing Post and Telecommunications University Press, October 2001.

Xinhua. "China Cancels Telephone Installation Charges." June 20, 2001.

———. "China Cuts Mobile Phone Fees." January 20, 2000.

———. "China Mobile Announces Reduction in Digital Line Leasing, Calling Charges." December 27, 2000.

———. "China Railcom, Satellite Interconnected." August 27, 2002.

———. "China's Railways Install Second Tele." March 30, 2000.

———. "China Telecom Initial Public Offering Now Fully Subscribed After Relaunch." November 7, 2002.

———. "China Unicom to Cut Telephone Fees." February 8, 2001.

———. "Government to Monitor Charges on Mobile Telecom Service." November 24, 1999.

———. "Information Ministry to Reorganize China Telecom." April 7, 1999.

———. "MII Plans to Lower Telecom Fees 'Significantly.'" December 30, 1998.

———. "Minister on Further Opening Telecom Market." April 2, 1999.

———. "Ministry of Railways Challenges China Telecom's Monopoly." May 26, 1999.

———. "PRC Railway Communications Links with China Telecom." September 23, 2001.

————. "Unicom Breaks Monopoly in Telephone Service." July 18, 1998.

————. "Zhu Rongji on Cutting Telecom Charges." March 15, 1999.

Xu Ke. "Dianxin: 3G huo fu" ["Telecommunications: 3G Disaster Fortune"]. *Caijing*, January 24, 2007.

Xu, Shaofeng, and Wenying Chen. "The Reform of Electricity Power in the People's Republic of China." *Energy Policy* 34 (2006): 2455–2465.

Xu Yan. "The Impact of the Regulatory Framework on Fixed-Mobile Interconnection Settlements: The Case of China and Hong Kong." *Telecommunications Policy* 25 (2001).

————, and Douglas Pitt. *Chinese Telecommunications Policy.* Boston: Artech House, 2002.

Xu Yi-chong. "A Powerhouse of Reform: Conversion from the Ministry of Electric Power to the State Power Corporation of China. *Australian Journal of Political Science* 36, no. 1 (2001): 123–143.

Yang, Dali. *Remaking the Chinese Leviathan: Market Transformation and the Politics of Governance.* Stanford, CA: Stanford University Press, 2004.

Yao, Kevin. "Ignored by Banks, China's Small Firms Make Pawnshops a Big Business." *Washington Post,* April 9, 2006.

Yearbook of China Transportation and Communications 2001. Beijing: China Transportation Yearbook Publishing House, 2001.

Yeung, Frederick. "Foreign Firms May Get Little from Bids for China Telecom." *South China Morning Post*, October 10, 2006.

Zhang, Anmin, and Hongmin Chen. "Evolution of China's Air Transport Development and Policy Towards International Liberalization." *Transportation Journal*, Spring 2003, 31–49.

Zhang Xinzhu, ed. *Zhongguo jichu sheshi chanye de guizhi gaige yu fazhan* [*Control, reform and development of China infrastructure industry*]. *Guojia xingzheng xueyuan chuban she* [*National Administration School Publishing House*]: Beijing, October 2002.

Zhao Huanxin. "Ministry Not to Open Internet Phone, Fax Sectors." *China Daily*, January 23, 1999.

————. "Phone Rates Reduction May Trigger Price War." *China Daily*, February 22, 2001.

Zhao, Yuezhi. *Media, Market, and Democracy in China: Between the Party Line and the Bottom Line.* Urbana: University of Illinois Press, 1998.

Zhongguo Tongxun She. "Ban on Foreign Investment in Telecommunications to Remain." As cited in BBC Summary of World Broadcasts, November 29, 1993.

Zhou Qiren. *Shuwang jingzheng: Zhongguo dianxin ye de guanzhi gaige he kaifang* [*Digital Network Competition: China Telecommunications Industry's*

Regulatory Reform and Liberalization] Beijing: Sanlian shenghuo dushu xinxi sanlian shudian [Sanlian Books], August 2000.

Zhu Fahua, Youfei Zheng, Xulin Gao, and Sheng Wang. "Environmental Impacts and Benefits of Regional Power Grid Interconnections for China." *Energy Policy* 33 (2005): 1797–1805.

Index

An f following a page number denotes a figure.